LISTENING

Student's Book

Beverly Fairfax and John Trzeciak

Longman

Other titles in the English for Academic Study series:

WHITE, R. and MCGOVERN, D.
Writing

TRZECIAK, J. and MACKAY, S. E.
Study Skills for Academic Writing

MCGOVERN, D., MATTHEWS, M. and MACKAY, S. E
Reading

FURNEAUX, C. and RIGNALL, M.
Speaking

Pearson Education Limited
Edinburgh Gate, Harlow
Essex CM20 2JE, England

www.longman.com

ISBN 0 582 42982 X
Third impression 2003

The publishers wish to state that they have made every effort to trace the copyright holders, but if they have inadvertently overlooked any they will be pleased to make the necessary arrangements at the first opportunity.

Packaged by Aldridge Press
Printed in Malaysia, PP

CONTENTS

ACKNOWLEDGEMENTS

Thanks are due to students, EAP teachers and other staff members at the Centre for Applied Language Studies, the University of Reading, for their contributions to the work. The invaluable assistance of the following, who helped with task design and evaluation, pedagogical analysis and/or the provision of notes, and recorded material, is gratefully acknowledged: John Alderman, Heather Bagley, Clare Booth, Colin Campbell, Clare Furneaux, Rita Green, Elizabeth Hallum, Paddy Harben, Pauline Jack, Joan McCormack, Anne Pallant, Amos Paran, Terry Phillips, Don Porter, Ros Richards, Jill Riley, Pauline Robinson, Gill Sturtridge, Clare Thomas, Paul Thompson, Alan Tonkyn, Paul Weller, Ron White, Eddie Williams. Helen Fraser is thanked for her help with many tasks, including transcribing some of the recordings, and Professor P.J. Roach, Dept. of Linguistic Science, for the phonemic transcriptions.

Among others who contributed to trialling, and whose feedback was vital in shaping the final version of the work, were: James Cooke, Rosalind Davies, Rosemary Dorey, Jim Gould, Irene Guy, Gordon Hart, John Lake, Wendy Mallas, Barry O'Sullivan, Alison Reynolds, John Slaght, Sue Weakley.

Members of the wider University community willingly participated in the provision of recorded material, and the enthusiasm and assistance of the following is gratefully acknowledged: Ms Tulay Balci (Dept. of Food Science and Technology), Professor J.A. Cantwell (Dept. of Economics), Dr. K.R. Dark (Dept. of Politics), Mr D.D. Malvern (Science and Technology Education), Professor F.P. McKenna (Dept. of Psychology), Dr. S. Nortcliff (Dept. of Soil Science), Professor H.E. Nursten (Dept. of Food Science and Technology), Professor M.J. Rolls (AERDD), Mr D.S. Shepherd (AERDD), Dr. K.P. Shine (Dept. of Meteorology), Dr. A.J.F. Warleigh (Dept. of Politics). Earlier work by Margaret Matthews is acknowledged as the impetus for some of these recordings.

For *Putting the military into print*, thanks are due to Profesor Julio Gimenez of Argentina and Licenciado Jorge Uribe of Colombia.

Without the unfailingly cheerful involvement of Paul Weller, the collection of the recorded material would have been a daunting task.

Particular thanks go to Ros Richards and Isobel Fletcher de Téllez for their constant support and encouragement throughout the project.

The photograph of Tulay Balci was taken by Best Color Studio, Ankara; the photograph of Elizabeth Hallum was taken by Philip Burbidge; the photograph of Professor Nursten was taken by Ian MacLean, of the University of Reading photographic unit. Dr M. Hanusova of the Czech Agricultural University, Prague, and J.E. Matthews, Agricultural Consultant, provided the photographs of Professor Rolls.

The photographs on pages 16 and 34 were taken by Katie Vandyke, © University of Reading.

The article *Take Two of Hydrogen and One of Oxygen* is based on information taken from 'The Battle for Water: Earth's most precious resource' in *Understanding Global Issues*, European Schoolbooks Publishing Ltd, Cheltenham.

The information in the article *S for Strategy, V for Victory*, is taken from Oxford, Rebecca L., 1990, *Language Learning Strategies: what every teacher should know* Newbury House, New York.

INTRODUCING THIS BOOK

Aims of the course

Understanding what you hear is like a jigsaw puzzle. If you have put all the pieces in the right place, you can see the picture very clearly.

If you can't make sense of any of the pieces, then you have no idea what the picture is supposed to be.

But if you have put some of the pieces in the right place, then you may be able to work out what the rest of the picture is like.

This course aims to give you as many pieces of the jigsaw puzzle as possible, and to show you that it is possible to work out the rest of the picture.

You are probably going to study at a college or university where the language of instruction is English. You might already have studied at that level in your own language, or you might be beginning academic study for the first time. Whatever experience you have had, you will probably find that some aspects of your lectures will be unfamiliar.

This course will help you to prepare for listening to lectures in English. As part of this preparation, you will be able to develop your note-taking skills. The course will also enable you to discover some of the features of spoken English.

Contents

There are nine units in the book. Each unit begins with a discussion. Your teacher may ask you to prepare for this discussion as a homework task. You should always try to relate the discussion questions to your own listening experience.

There are a number of tasks in each unit. Some of them are pre-listening tasks to do before you listen to the cassette tape, to make your listening more effective. Sometimes you will do a task while you listen – perhaps to take notes, to listen for some specific information, or to pay close attention to the particular words the speaker uses. You will do other tasks after you have listened to the tape. The tasks in each unit provide opportunities for both individual and group work. The tape icon ⊙⊙ indicates when you should listen to the tape.

On the tape you will hear interviews with lecturers and students, extracts from lectures and some complete short lectures.

There are 'Interludes' after Units 3 and 6. The Interludes will give you a different kind of listening practice. In an Interlude unit you will listen to a short talk and complete a variety of tasks.

There are two further recordings (*Conflict Management* and *Archaeology*) which may be used for extra listening and note-taking practice. Each lasts for about thirteen minutes.

There are transcripts of all the recorded material at the end of this book. You may think that the punctuation in some of these transcripts is rather strange – there are more commas than you would expect to see in written English. This is because the transcripts try to show some of the pauses which occur in natural speech. You will also see the speakers' hesitations and repetitions, which are a normal part of spoken English.

Each unit contains 'Soundbites'. These are hints and reminders to help you to make progress in your listening. Pay attention to these and always make a note of any interesting or useful ideas that you learn in class work and discussions. Review these notes often.

You will also see a box labelled 'The Reflective Learner' at the end of each unit. This is designed to draw your attention to the main aspects of listening which you have been working on in the unit.

Keeping a Learner Diary

If you have used the *Speaking* book in this series, you will know that research suggests that you will develop your language skills more effectively if you think about your learning. This book provides you with an opportunity to keep a Learner Diary at the end of each unit. You should keep a special notebook or file for this purpose.

When you finish each unit, look at the points mentioned in the Reflective Learner box. Note down in your Learner Diary your thoughts about what you have learnt. You could ask yourself:

- Do I understand the aims of this unit?
- Do I think the work in this unit has helped me?
- How does the work in this unit relate to my particular needs?
- What am I going to do now to practise what I have just learnt?

You will also find specific questions to help you with your Learner Diary entry.

Try to find ten or fifteen minutes at the end of each unit to complete your Learner Diary. You do not have to answer all the questions – choose the ones that seem most relevant to you. You can also write about other aspects of your listening that are important to you at the time.

Your Learner Diary is for yourself, not for anyone else to look at. You need not worry about writing in perfect sentences. Your diary is not a writing exercise – it is an opportunity to think and reflect. You can keep it private, or you can share parts of it with your teacher or a fellow student. If you share it with your teacher, he or she will learn more about you, and will be able to offer you further guidance and advice about your listening.

At the end of the course, when you read your diary right through from beginning to end, you may be surprised and delighted to see how much progress you have made.

Over the page is an example of the sort of thing you could write in your Learner Diary:

Friday, 15 th
Unit 6

I have improved. When I started, I had a lot
of trouble listening and taking notes at the
same time. Now I can usually write down most
of the main ideas.

I tried to make diagram notes this time. I've
never used that style before. I found it hard.
I'll borrow a taped lecture and practise on
Wednesday afternoon.

Some words of advice

- Be a flexible listener. Always try to make sense of what you hear, even if there are words you do not understand.

- Be an enthusiastic learner of words. Aim to increase your vocabulary as much as possible. Reading in your chosen academic subject will help you to learn more about how people express its concepts and ideas. Make use of a good English-English dictionary: firstly, to check meanings and secondly, to check the pronunciation of words so that you recognise them when you hear them.

- Be an active and interactive learner by working with other students and sharing your views and experience. Working with other students will help you to develop your confidence and your understanding of the listening process.

UNIT

1 LISTENING

In this unit you will:

- think about listening in your own language
- think about listening in English
- hear an international student talking about listening to lectures
- learn what some researchers believe about listening in a second language
- try taking notes

DISCUSSION

Thinking about language

1. What language do you speak at home? Do you use any other languages in your daily life?
2. What do the following terms mean?
   mother tongue
   foreign language
   second language
   native speaker of English
   non-native speaker of English
3. When we use language, we *speak, listen, read* and *write*. In what ways are the first two similar? In what ways are the last two similar? Can you see any other way of grouping them?

TASK 1

1.1   Get into a group with other students and discuss the questions in the box on the next page.

1. What do you enjoy about listening to English?

2. How much experience have you had of listening to English (both academic and non-academic)?

3. What are your feelings about listening to English at college or university?

4. Are there any non-academic listening situations in your own language which you have found difficult? Why? What did you do about your difficulties?

5. How much experience have you had of listening to academic talk in your own language?

6. How important are lectures in a course of study in your country? Is it possible to be a successful student only on the basis of attending lectures?

7. In your own language, which do you remember better – what you have heard or what you have read? Can you say why?

8. In what ways do you think understanding an academic lecture may be different from reading an academic book or article on the same subject?

9. What can you do to make listening to a lecture easier?

1.2 Prepare a brief, organised summary of the important or most interesting ideas from your group, and present this report to the rest of the class.

TASK 2

2.1 You are going to listen to an interview with Tulay Balci, a Turkish student studying for a PhD. She is discussing her experience of listening to lectures.

Afterwards, you will decide which of the following statements are true, according to what you hear in the interview.

Read the statements first.

Tulay Balci, from Turkey

1. *Tulay thought that the lectures were too long.*
2. *All the lecturers were boring.*
3. *Tulay thinks it's easier to understand a lecture if you know something about the subject.*
4. *She didn't learn very much from her lectures.*
5. *She did some reading before every lecture.*
6. *The handouts were useful.*
7. *Most lecturers used a microphone.*
8. *Tulay thinks that discussing the work with other students is not a very good idea.*
9. *She appreciated the lecturers who tried to make the students laugh.*
10. *Tulay would like to be a university lecturer.*

2.2 Cover the statements in 2.1 with a piece of paper, so that you cannot read them while you are listening.

Now listen to the interview, and take notes to help you choose the true statements. If you find it hard to take notes while you listen, just concentrate on listening, and make a few notes afterwards.

2.3 Use the notes you took in 2.2 to help you decide which statements in 2.1 are true.

2.4 Check your answers with other students and discuss the following questions:

- *Were there words you have never heard before? Did you hear a word but think it was a different word?*
- *Were you able to work out any of the words that you missed? If so, how did you work them out?*
- *Were there any questions which you were unable to answer? If so, why couldn't you answer them?*

2.5 Tulay spoke about four aspects of listening to lectures:

- *the students*
- *the subject matter*
- *the lecturers*
- *the conditions under which listening takes place*

Use your notes to find at least one point that she made about each.

> • *If it's hard at the moment for you to listen and take notes at the same time, listen to the tape first, and write your notes afterwards.*

TASK 3

3.1 You are going to listen to a talk about listening in a second language. The talk connects the ancient Greek word *strategia* with listening strategies. Do you think that a listening strategy might be a positive or negative concept?

Listen and take notes at the same time if you can. Your notes should remind you of what the speaker says about:

- *the connection between the Greek word* strategia *and the English word* strategy,
- *the different kinds of listening strategies.*

There is some more information about this on page 76 that you might find useful.

3.2 If you didn't take notes while you were listening, then write brief notes now. It does not matter if you write only a few words.

If you did take notes, check them with a partner to see if you both wrote down similar ideas.

3.3 Look at your notes and see if they help you to answer the following questions:

1. *For the Ancient Greeks, did* strategia *have a positive or a negative feeling?*
2. *What is the connection between the Greek understanding of* strategia *and listening strategies?*
3. *According to the speaker, what is mental processing?*
4. *When you wonder if you have understood something, what sort of strategy are you using?*

3.4 Work with a group of other students. Look at this list of listening strategies. Which ones do you think you already use? Note down the strategies used most often by your group.

- *taking notes while you listen*
- *listening for key words and phrases*

- *writing about your progress and problems in a diary*
- *trying to identify the different parts of a lecture*
- *thinking about your reason for listening*
- *reading before listening*
- *making conscious connections with what you know already*
- *listening for key ideas*
- *guessing what an unknown word might mean or refer to*
- *discussing a lecture with other students afterwards*
- *consciously trying to listen in English instead of translating into your mother tongue*

Can anyone in your group suggest any other strategies?

3.5   Report your results to the rest of the class and find out if other groups seem to use the same strategies as your group.

THE REFLECTIVE LEARNER

Re-read the introduction to this book so that you understand how keeping a Learner Diary regularly can help you.

In this unit you have reflected on your experience of listening to lectures in English and your mother tongue. You have also thought about listening strategies that you have used, or that you might use in future.

You can become a better listener by thinking about the process of listening.

Questions for your diary
1.   What do you think you will find easy when you are listening to lectures on your course?
2.   What new strategies will you try to use?

UNIT 2 WHAT THE BRAIN DOES WITH LANGUAGE

In this unit you will:

- think about making sense of what you hear
- discover what makes it hard for you to recognise the words you hear

DISCUSSION

Thinking about what the brain does with language

1. Say a sentence quickly in your own language. Would someone who didn't understand your language be able to say how many words there are in your sentence? Can you suggest why or why not?
2. Do you find it difficult to know where spoken words begin and end in English? Can you suggest why or why not?
3. Words which sound the same (such as *one/won* or *wore/war* in English) are called 'homonyms'. When you hear a word like this, what helps you to make the right choice?

TASK 1

1.1   Imagine you are listening to the lecture or seminar described below. You can recognise some of the words, but not all of them. The balloons on the right show the words and sounds that you think the lecturer said. Speak the sentences aloud and try to work out what the lecturer actually said in each case.

a lecture on photography in the nineteenth century

thcustomev hangcullering photos was widely practist

a seminar on the building laws that make sure disabled people are able to get into buildings

offissesneed tbe easy fpeeplin wheel chairs tgetin to

a lecture on the British monarchy

Elizabeth became kweenin ninety fifty too onthdethiva father

a seminar on International Development

theach passing year, the incum gap between the havsen the havnots increase is alarmingly

1.2   Many researchers believe that when you are listening you go through various stages to create meaning out of the sounds you hear. Look at the following four stages:

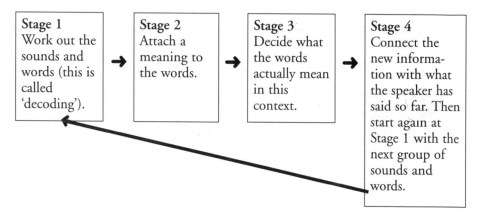

Stage 1	Stage 2	Stage 3	Stage 4
Work out the sounds and words (this is called 'decoding').	Attach a meaning to the words.	Decide what the words actually mean in this context.	Connect the new information with what the speaker has said so far. Then start again at Stage 1 with the next group of sounds and words.

1.3   Listen to the tape of another four sentences from the same lectures and seminars:

    1. from the photography lecture,
    2. from the seminar on building laws,
    3. from the monarchy lecture,
    4. from the International Development seminar.

With a partner, try to work out what each speaker is saying.

Which stage in the model were you working at for each sentence?

Soundbite

- *It is important to be able to recognise words very quickly. If you don't know enough words, you will spend too long on Stage 1, and you will miss the meaning.*
- *So – learn words!*

TASK 2

2.1 Read the following summary which a student wrote from the notes he took on a lecture on Global Climate Change. It contains one factual error. Try to decide what the error is.

> Global climate change
> (KPS 2 March)
>
> Since 1860 the world's temperature has increased by 0.5 degrees because of human activities such as global war and using gases which affect the atmosphere.

2.2 Discuss the questions in the box below.

1. What is the error in the summary?
2. What word do you think the lecturer actually used?
3. Why do you think the student thought he heard a different word?
4. How could the student have recognised that his notes were wrong?

TASK 3

3.1 Read the following transcript from a lecture on language use in society. The extract comes from the middle of the lecture.

Do not worry about the blanks in the transcript at this stage. Just try to get an idea of what the lecturer is saying. When you have read the script, listen to the tape and write down the missing words. There may be one or several words to write down.

> Right, O.K. Erm, now, it's, erm, often said that when two English people meet, they learn a lot about each other just by___(1)___, and uttering a few words, I mean just a sentence even. Erm, so for example, let's think, people on a train, in a railway carriage. Let's imagine one's asking the other to open the window, well, or maybe close the window, 5 perhaps that's a, a more normal situation. Now, there's no ___(2)___ way of doing this, so in asking, one is, always, revealing something about oneself.

You can ask ___(3)___, can't you? 'Could you possibly close the window please? It's a bit cold in here.' 'Oi, shut the window.' Now obviously, first of all, one's ___(4)___ to the other person is shown here. Now that might be deliberate. One form is more polite, the other's less polite. Another point is that pronunciation shows one's ___(5)___ . So, for example, we have Scottish, northern, London, and other accents. `10` `15`

All of this, that I've talked about so far, can be found in other countries and with other languages, so that people can be polite, or impolite, people's accents ___(6)___ where they come from.

But in England, we've got something else. Let's listen again. 'Could you possibly close the window please. I... , it's a bit cold in here.' 'Oi, close the window!' The first is BBC English, ___(7)___, the second, cockney, or something similar. What do these show? Well these show social class. So as well as regional origin, one is showing one's social class. `20`

3.2 You're going to hear another extract from the lecture. This time some of the gaps are quite close together, and you will have to write more words in each gap. Do you think this will make it harder for you to write the words?

First, read the text, to get the overall idea of what the lecturer is saying. Then listen and write down the correct words.

Right, let's take the situation where we have, say, erm an American, a German and a Japanese in the railway carriage, and they are being asked to close the window. Now all of them have good English. They can understand that the English person wants the window closed, but ___(1)___ all the other information, th... , the social information? ___(2)___ they probably don't. `5`

So, ___(3)___, Germans for example are seen by the British, erm, especially the English, ___(4)___. Why is this? Well, Germans don't usually say 'please'. ___(5)___ direct commands. Americans can also seem to British people to be a bit abrupt. Whereas British people, erm, especially the English, well, they can seem horribly obsequious and ___(6)___. 'Hey, gosh, why are they being so incredibly polite?' Well the English person just thinks he, or she, is being normally polite. The Japanese or the German again would have a ___(7)___, of what the English person is doing. None of them would necessarily pick up the social origin of the speaker. I mean, they wouldn't know how the `10` `15` different social classes are typically, sort of, indicated ___(8)___ people speak.

So what, what are we, what's happening in all this? What's going on? Well, really, what we're doing, ___(9)___. We're talking about how ways of speaking English are ___(10)___ in the culture of the community. And what do we mean by culture? Well, we mean a set of expected ways of behaving ___(11)___. 20

3.3 Check with other students to see if you have written the same words in the blanks.

If you have written different words, think about the reasons for this. Ask yourself the following questions:

- *Were there words you have never heard before?*
- *Did you hear a word but think it was a different word?*
- *Did you have any problems working out how many words to write in each gap?*
- *If you missed any words, did you try to work them out or did you skip them?*
- *Did the longer, closer gaps in 3.2 make it harder to identify the correct words?*

THE REFLECTIVE LEARNER

In this unit you have reflected on your awareness of how the brain manages language.

When your brain recognises words automatically, you become a better listener.

Questions for your diary
1. How can you increase the speed with which you recognise the words you hear?
2. What will you do to increase your vocabulary?

UNIT

3 *LECTURES*

In this unit you will:

- learn about different styles of lecturing and the role of lectures and seminars in a course of study
- learn about the structure of lectures

DISCUSSION

Thinking about lectures

1. Think of lectures which you have attended either in English or in your own language. What was the lecturer's role? What was the student's role?
2. If you are familiar with the structure of a lecture, this can help you to understand it better. Can you think why?
3. In some subjects, a common pattern in a lecture is to present the theories that researchers have proposed, and then to report some data which prove or disprove those theories. In others, the lecturer first presents a problem or a weakness, analyses what caused the problem, and then proposes a solution.

    Can you comment on the structure of any lectures you have heard? Have you noticed different structures for lectures in different subjects? Are there sometimes different structures for lectures in the same course?

TASK 1

1.1   You are going to hear an interview with Mr Derek Shepherd, a lecturer in Agricultural Extension. In the interview, he explains the role of lecturers and describes lectures and seminars in his department (called 'AERDD').

*Students in
a lecture*

Before you listen, read the following phrases which you will hear in the interview.
Decide if the meaning given for each phrase is likely to be accurate in the context
of the interview.

1. a broad framework
    a comprehensive way of looking at a subject

2. the transmission of factual information
    a news broadcast

3. a presentation from a highly structured script
    a lecture in which the lecturer uses detailed, prepared notes

4. interactive and participatory
    providing an opportunity at the end for students to ask questions

5. a two-way process
    a lecture given by two different people

6. enhance our understanding of the subject area
    make a contribution to everyone's developing knowledge

7. they can devise their own understanding of the subject area
    they can ignore what the lecturer says

8. an issue that they're facing in their work
   a situation they have to deal with at work

9. how they've dealt with them
   what they've done about them

10. most of them cope with them
    most of them have problems

11. a key idea
    the answer to a question

12. a piece of the literature
    an extract from a book or research article

TASK 2

2.1 After you have listened to the interview you will try to organise your notes under the following headings:

- *What students have to listen to*
- *What lecturers want students to take from lectures*
- *Different styles of lectures*
- *How students cope with lectures and seminars*
- *The use of handouts and visual aids*

Now listen to the interview and take notes.

2.2 Reorganise your notes under the headings listed in 2.1.

2.3 Check your notes with other students and discuss the following questions:

- *Were you all able to take notes in all five areas? If not, which areas did you miss, and why?*
- *Have you all written down the same information? If not, why do you think your information is different?*
- *Were there words you have never heard before? Did you hear a word but think it was a different word?*
- *Was there anything that made it particularly difficult for you to understand the interview?*
- *Which information did you find the most interesting? Did you find any of the information surprising or exciting? Did any of it worry you?*

TASK 3

3.1 To help you how to learn to understand important words, you will read and hear an extract from the interview again.

Read through the extract. Do not worry about the blanks in the transcript at this stage.

Interviewer: So within this kind of interactive lecture, there's a, there's a role for the students to make their own contribution and in some way to ___(1)___? Or is that perhaps taking that point a little bit too far?

Mr Shepherd: Erm, th... that can happen, erm, if, er, this q... the questions that the students ask will, erm, allow the lecturer to use that   5
to ___(2)___, er, the material that, er, he, the lecturer is trying to address. And, indeed if, if, er, this, it may move, it may mean that perhaps a lecturer hasn't q... perhaps covered quite the ___(3)___ that they were intending to, in that period. Er, but they will have a frame-work that they're trying to work to. If they don't complete it in that   10
period er, because of this interactive process, then they will, then they will try and make that up in, at a, at a, ___(4)___. But it is, er, the lecturer still is intending to erm, cover a certain amount of material, and erm, if he doesn't manage it because of that interactive process then it'll be added into the next session. But it's ___(5)___.   15

Interviewer: Would you like to talk a little bit about the advantages or disadvantages of one or other of those styles, the, the style which uses a more prepared script, compared to the more interactive style where there is more place for the students to ___(6)___?

Mr Shepherd: Erm, yes, I suppose, I haven't really thought about this before, but erm, I suppose that erm, the advantage of the interactive   20
style is that er, there's more opportunities, er, for the, for the student to ___(7)___ with the, the concepts and the theories that the, the lecturer is, is trying to erm, present, and gives them a sense of, erm, that the learning is, is a two-way process, that it isn't simply, erm, the lecturer has all the ideas, ___(8)___, but that students themselves erm, have, er,   25
experiences which, erm, can help to illustrate those ideas and concepts, but perhaps hadn't thought about them in that way until, until they attended that, that lecture. The, the more formal one, erm, perhaps has the advantage of erm, being able to, if you like, to keep to the frame-work, to ___(9)___. Erm, and I think that's probably also satisfactory,   30
providing the lecturer has left some time for erm, questions. But I think it, it ___(10)___ between the role of the lecturer and, and the role of the, of, of the student. One is a, a giver and ___(11)___. And I

think, at, at a, at post-graduate level, certainly at master's level, erm, we're, we're not talking about ___(12)___. These are people that have, the students who have a lot of, er, a lot of knowledge and experience that can, erm, enhance our understanding of the subject area.

35

3.2 Now listen to the extract and try to write down the missing word or words. There may be one or several words to write down.

3.3 Check your answers with other students.

TASK 4

4.1 Listen to an extract from a lecture on intercultural communication. What is the style of this lecture?

Think about what you heard in the interview in 2.1 and discuss the following questions.

1. Why does the lecturer ask the first student about Ireland?
2. How does the lecturer make use of the second student's statement – 'It's the subversive Irish again,' ?
3. How does he keep control of the content of the lecture?
4. Can you think of any problems that you might have in this kind of lecture?

TASK 5

5.1 You will hear Elizabeth talking to a group of students about her own experiences as a student. She went back to university to do post-graduate work many years after she had finished her under-graduate work. She had problems with her lectures, and she describes how she solved these problems.

Look on the next page at four possible ways of organising the talk. If you were asked to give a talk like this, which plan would you choose? Why?

Elizabeth talking about returning to study.

19

Plan 1

- Whether her solution worked.
- The listening problems she had when she returned to university to do an MA.
- What she had been doing before she returned.
- How she solved the problems.

Plan 2

- What she had been doing before she returned to university.
- The listening problems she had when she started her MA.
- How she solved the problems.
- Whether her solution worked.

Plan 3

- The solution she discovered to the problems of listening.
- Whether her solution worked.
- Why she found listening difficult.
- What she had been doing before she returned to do her MA.

Plan 4

- Why she found listening difficult when she returned to do an MA.
- What she had been doing before she returned to do her MA.
- Whether her solution worked.
- How she solved the problems.

5.2 Now listen to Elizabeth talking and note down the language that signals her plan. Does she use the plan that you would have chosen?

5.3 Listen again and take notes on:

1. Elizabeth's problems, and
2. the breakthrough she made in her listening.

From your notes, can you say what advice Elizabeth might give to the students she was talking to?

Soundbite

- *If you know what the purpose of a lecture is and you recognise its structure, you will understand the lecture better.*
- *In some kinds of lecture, you will be expected to answer questions and share your experiences.*

THE REFLECTIVE LEARNER

In this unit you have heard about the purpose of lectures and about different lecturing styles. You have reflected on your own experience and expectations of lectures.

Knowing what a lecturer is trying to do in a lecture and what you are expected to contribute, can help you to understand the lecture better.

Questions for your diary
1. What do you think about the lecturing styles you have heard about?
2. How confident are you about participating in interactive lectures?
3. If you are going to start studying your own subject soon, what can you do now to find out about lecturing styles on your course?

1 PUTTING THE MILITARY INTO PRINT

TASK 1

1.1   Look at this list of names and answer the questions:

> *Pablo Neruda*
> *Isabel Allende*
> *Mario Benedetti*
> *Gabriel Garcia Marquez*
> *Jorge Borges*

1. What continent do all these people come from?
2. They all share the same profession. Do you know what it is?
3. In the 1960s and 1980s most of them lived in countries with military regimes. What is a military regime?

TASK 2

2.1   Listen to the first extract and identify the countries which Borges, Allende and Benedetti come from.

2.2   Listen to the extract again and choose the correct information from the following list:

1. *Most countries had returned to democracy by the early eighties.*
2. *Before the military governments took power, the countries had been unstable.*

3. *The speaker believes that the citizens of these countries like having military governments.*
4. *The speaker says that he will also talk about writers from Colombia and Peru.*
5. *During the military regimes, some people became poor.*

2.3   What consequences of the military regimes did the three writers deal with in their work?

TASK 3

3.1   What do the following words and expressions mean?

(a) aristocratic
(b) humanitarian
(c) suffer the consequences
(d) ordinary people
(e) social oppression
(f) a human rights supporter
(g) people with high ideals
(h) freedom of speech
(i) the voice of the oppressed
(j) exile
(k) longing

3.2   Listen to the rest of the talk and take notes so that you can answer the following questions:

1. *According to the speaker, what was the effect of the military regimes on the 'upper classes'?*
2. *What was unusual about Borges?*
3. *When the speaker mentions Borges' writing, which kind of writing does he discuss, for example, poems, plays, novels, short stories or essays?*
4. *What does the speaker mean when he says that Borges' writing was 'a mirror to poverty and social oppression'?*
5. *How are Allende's themes different from those of Borges?*
6. *Is Allende a novelist, a playwright, a poet or a film director?*
7. *Why does the speaker see Benedetti as 'the voice of the oppressed?'*
8. *What are the major themes of Benedetti's writing?*

3.3   Share your notes with other students and answer the questions.

2 DEFINITELY NOT ENGLAND

TASK 1

1.1 There is one area missing from this map of the United Kingdom. Can you name the missing area and the people who come from that area? Where should this area be on the map?

1.2 What do you know about the area you have just added to the map?

TASK 2

2.1 You are going to hear a lecturer speaking about the area you have just identified. In the introduction to his talk, he uses the following expressions:

    (a) a common border
    (b) very much tied up with that of England
    (c) the Act of Union
    (d) the decline of national identity
    (e) the nineteenth century
    (f) a sudden resurgence in nationalism

When you have read the expressions, discuss the points you think the lecturer will make about the connections between England and the area he is describing.

2.2 Listen to the first extract to see how accurate you were.

TASK 3

3.1 Discuss what the following words and expressions mean or refer to:

    (a) moorlands and valleys
    (b) went into considerable decline
    (c) virtually disappeared
    (d) silicon chips
    (e) one of the most distinctive features
    (f) a first language
    (g) a medium of instruction
    (h) to pursue a degree
    (i) a double-edged sword
    (j) political autonomy
    (k) certainly of advantage
    (l) fallout from the Chernobyl accident
    (m) contaminated

3.2 Listen to the second extract and take notes under the following eight headings. Leave out any information which does not relate to these headings. Your notes will not be complete at the end of this extract.

Agriculture	Industry	The language
• In the south • In the north	• In the past • Now • Tourism	• As a first language • Its place in education • The advantages of speaking it

Compare your notes with a partner's to see if you both heard the same things and took similar notes.

3.3 Listen to the final extract and complete your notes. Then check with a partner as you did in 3.2.

TASK 4

4.1 Review your notes and decide which information would be useful to you if you were going to write an essay entitled:

Britain may be proud of its past, but is it sure of its future?

Be prepared to share your ideas with the rest of the class and to justify your choice.

UNIT 4

INTRODUCTIONS AND SIGNPOST LANGUAGE

In this unit you will:

- look at how an introduction can help you to understand a lecture better
- learn how lecturers can guide you through a lecture

DISCUSSION

Thinking about introductions and signpost language

1. What do you expect to hear in the introduction to a lecture?
2. Think of lectures you have heard. Did the lecturers try to make the structure of the lecture obvious to students? If so, how?
3. What do you think 'signpost language' means?

TASK 1

1.1   Look at these words spoken by a lecturer at the beginning of his lecture:

> Many of you come from cities which are rather polluted. We've been hearing on the radio over the past few days about quite bad air pollution in London, for example. I'm not concerned immediately with that kind of city-scale pollution, so the pollution which is confined to a city, I'm thinking more, more on the global scale about the way human activity may be changing the global atmosphere.

Look at these notes taken by two students.

Student 1 wrote:

> Dealing with:
> (London) Concerned with city-scale pollution –
> incrd. global pollution

Student 2 wrote:

> Not city scale pollut^n but general
> global changes
> General overview: human activity
> changing atmosphere

Which student didn't understand how the lecturer was going to look at pollution?

1.2 Listen to the introduction on tape. Why do you think the student made a mistake? Which words in the introduction signal what the lecturer will talk about?

TASK 2

2.1 Read the items in the left-hand column. They show what lecturers commonly do in introductions.

Match each item with a statement from a lecture from the right hand column. All the statements are taken from introductions to lectures.

What lecturers do

(a) Indicate that they are referring back to previous lectures and are reminding students of their content

(b) Show how the lecture fits in to a series – 'position' the lecture

(c) Preview the content or structure of the lecture

(d) Refer to research in the subject – this often includes mentioning specific reading material

(e) Draw attention to any background information they are providing to give a context for the lecture

(f) Explain or justify the relevance of a subject or an approach, particularly at the beginning of a series of lectures

(g) Distribute handouts or mention how they will be used in the lecture

(h) Limit the scope of the lecture

(i) Explain the lecturer's own involve-ment with the subject

Lecturer statements

1. *Why are we looking at the subject in this particular way?*

2. *I'm planning to take a historical rather than a contemporary view of this.*

3. *Pollock and Greer have been the leading lights in the field for quite some time now and they've shaped the way most people are currently thinking.*

4. *My own interest stems from some work I did in the early eighties.*

5. *You'll see notes on this on the sheets I gave out earlier, and I'll be referring to those as we go along.*

6. *Today we're on the last of the sessions looking at the impact of the Cold War in Asia.*

7. *That's just to put you in the picture.*

8. *I'll be describing some of these theories and then suggesting to you that there are other ways of looking at this whole question.*

9. *We looked at some of this last time.*

2.2   Listen on the tape to the introductions to three lectures.

 Identify which aspects from the list in 2.1 each lecturer appears to be using (at least two for each introduction). The lecture topics are:

    1. *Britain and European Monetary Union*
    2. *Globalisation*
    3. *Soil Science*

2.3   Listen to the introduction to a lecture on eyewitness testimony[1].

---

[1] 'eyewitness testimony' is evidence given in court by someone who saw a crime being committed

Try to identify how this introduction is different from the previous three. What do you think the lecturer might do after this introduction?

TASK 3

3.1 You are going to listen to the introduction to the first economics lecture of the year. There will be seven lectures in the first term. As you listen, decide which lecture or lectures will deal with each of these topics:

(a) money demand
(b) aggregate supply
(c) investment demand
(d) IS-LM analysis
(e) the history of the development of macro-economics
(f) consumption function

3.2 Listen to the tape again and note down any information that will help you to answer the following questions:

> 1. How will the work that students have already done in their first year help them in this course?
> 2. What does the lecturer intend to do in Terms 2 and 3?

Discuss the questions with other students.

3.3 Using the list in 2.1, discuss what the economics lecturer is doing in this introduction, and why.

Soundbite

- *Listen carefully to the introductions to all your lectures. This may help you to understand the lectures better and take better notes.*

TASK 4

4.1 After the introduction, lecturers will move on to the main body of the lecture. One way of classifying what they do in the main body is as follows:

1. Present the content
2. Organise the content
3. Comment on the content
4. Interact with students

Read this list and classify the items into the four categories above.

(a) ask and answer questions
(b) come back to the main topic
(c) delay an idea until later in the lecture
(d) describe theories
(e) end a section
(f) evaluate (give an opinion about the value or validity of) a theory or an idea
(g) give data and information
(h) give examples
(i) give instructions
(j) introduce an example
(k) indicate a change of focus
(l) refer to an idea already mentioned
(m) report research
(n) summarise what has been said or indicate a summary
(o) introduce an evaluation
(p) outline the content of the next lecture or next section

4.2   The language you will hear in lectures depends on the subject. It is obviously not possible to predict every sentence lecturers might use, particularly to *present the content*. However, the language used to *organise* and *comment on the content*, and to *interact with students*, is more restricted and perhaps easier to predict, even if there are many possible variations.

The following expressions of this sort ('signpost language') have been taken from various lectures.

Read the sentences and phrases on the next page and try to classify them. Sometimes there may be more than one possibility.

1. *What I want to do now is outline the background to the research.*
2. *Clearly this is only one approach to the problem, and perhaps not even the best one.*
3. *Let me give you a couple of examples.*
4. *Anyway, that's rather beside the point.*
5. *It's evident that this is not entirely satisfactory.*
6. *So those are two different ways of looking at the same problem.*
7. *Now, let's look back at the first point I made.*
8. *Let's focus for a moment on the second law.*
9. *Would you like to have a look at those articles before next time?*
10. *I would suggest that neither of these theories accounts for the phenomenon.*

There are some more signpost expressions on page 77.

Soundbite

- *Signpost words can help you to follow the structure of a lecture.*
- *The organising words you will hear in lectures are often very different from the text organising words used in writing, although their purpose may be the same.*

THE REFLECTIVE LEARNER

In this unit you have studied introductions to lectures and thought about how lecturers might guide you through a lecture. You have seen that good introductions and effective signposting are a feature of many lectures.

If the material in a lecture is new or difficult, listening carefully to the introduction and the signposts might help you to follow the lecture better.

Questions for your diary
1. Are the introductions you have heard different from introductions you are used to? If so, how are they different?
2. How will you become more familiar with the language that lecturers use to organise and to comment on the content of a lecture?

5 NOTE-*taking*

In this unit you will:

- think about your note-taking
- think about what makes effective notes
- look at different styles of notes
- have the opportunity to try out different styles of note-taking

DISCUSSION

Thinking about note taking

1. Do you always take notes in lectures? If you don't always take notes, why not, and what do you do instead? What do you do afterwards?
2. Look at the following descriptions of listeners. The descriptions may help you to see how your experience as a listener might affect your note-taking. Which one seems to describe you at the moment?

A less experienced listener
- You use most of your cognitive capacity ('brain space') to decode. You have to concentrate on decoding (i.e. working out the words).
- You cannot take many notes; you may write down words because you understand them, even if they are not necessarily important words.

A more experienced listener
- You can select and record information.
- You are able to note key-words and phrases and record some of the ideas.

A very experienced listener
- You manage to analyse the content and re-order the incoming information.
- You can choose from a wide range of appropriate note-taking strategies to record data and summarise the concepts being developed.

3. When you take notes, what sort of notes do you take? Why do you use that method? Are you satisfied with what you do? Why or why not?
4. What abbreviations and symbols do you use when you take notes?

TASK 1

1.1 What is the purpose of a university? Is it for training (acquiring defined skills to use in predictable situations) or education (acquiring understanding to use in unpredictable situations)?

How do you think getting your degree will improve your life?

Students talking about their work

1.2 You are going to listen to an extract from a lecture on higher education. The lecturer is discussing the role of a university, and he has just asked, 'But what actually is it for and should we be in some sense useful?' ('We' means 'universities'.) During this section of the lecture, he refers to three overhead transparencies (OHTs).

First, read these two OHTs:

OHT 1

> **Spirit of enquiry — knowledge for knowledge's sake?**
>
> **Cultural reservoirs — in the museum of history?**
>
> **Cultural purity — gate-keepers of the truth?**
>
> **Pursuit of excellence — only the best for the best?**
>
> **Service to the community — who is the community?**

OHT 2

A body of knowledge, enshrined in a university faculty and embodied in a series of authoritative volumes, is the result of much prior intellectual activity. To instruct someone in these disciplines is not a matter of getting him to commit results to mind. Rather, it is to teach him to participate in the process that makes possible the establishment of knowledge. We teach a subject not to produce little living libraries on that subject, but rather to get a student to think mathematically for himself, to consider matters as an historian does, to take part in the process of knowledge-getting. Knowledge is a process, not a product.

(*Towards a Theory of Instruction*, J.S. Bruner, Harvard University Press, 1966)

What do you think the lecturer will say about the purpose of a university?

1.3 Now read the third OHT, which suggests that people who do not appreciate art have the potential to damage their environment. (Note that the expression 'in after life' is used here to mean 'life after school or university'.)

OHT 3

'While it will of course be readily admitted that all are not equally gifted aesthetically, even pupils with no special skill in Art may gain much from associating with those who are producing fine work. By such contact, something of the interest which makes for understanding and appreciation is readily communicated. Such pupils may in after life attain positions of influence in industry, in educational affairs, or in public life, in which if they lack aesthetic development, they may prove a danger to the community. ... They do constitute a danger, and by their indifference to natural and architectural beauty, may be the means of permanently disfiguring a countryside or a city.'

(*Curriculum*, Scottish Council for Research in Education, 1931)

Why do you think the lecturer uses this quotation?

1.4 Now listen to the extract on the tape and take notes in your preferred style. When the lecturer reads from each OHT, make sure you look at the correct one.

1.5 Take two minutes to review your notes, filling in any gaps and checking to see if your notes make sense.

Compare your notes with those of other students and discuss the following questions:

- *Are there any style or content differences between your notes?*
- *How did you all decide what to write down?*
- *Did anyone copy from the OHT and if so, why?*

1.6 Read these criteria for 'successful' notes, and see how many of these features appear in your group's notes:

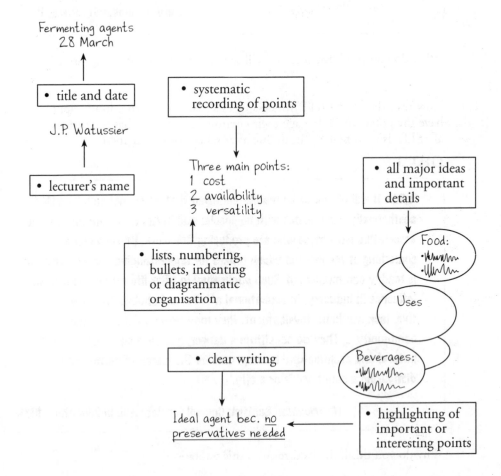

TASK 2

2.1 Look at these three OHTs. They contain graphs which the lecturer refers to in the next part of his lecture.

What connection do you think the lecturer might make between *education* and *life expectancy*?

OHT 4

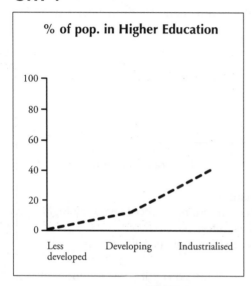

OHT 5

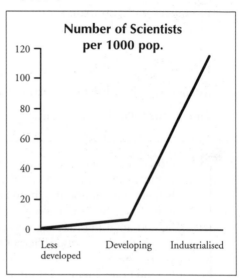

OHT 6

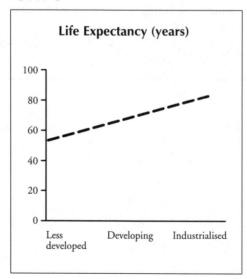

2.2 Now listen to the next extract from the lecture and continue the notes you
started in 1.4. When the lecturer describes each graph, look at the relevant OHT.

2.3 Take two minutes to review your notes, adding anything else you think is
important.

Compare your notes with those of other students. Are your notes different this
time?

From your notes, can you say whether the lecturer agrees with the idea that a
university should be useful?

2.4 Look closely at the notes on the next two pages, which were taken by two
listeners who heard the same extracts as you.

Discuss the following questions:

> **?**
> 1. How is each set of notes organised? Does the organisation help you to
>   identify the lecturer's main ideas?
> 2. Is there enough/too much information?
> 3. How have the listeners highlighted important points? Have they high-
>   lighted anything they want to check later?
> 4. What similarities and differences are there between these notes and
>   yours?
> 5. Do the notes include information from the OHTs? If so, is it important
>   information?
> 6. Have the listeners just copied down a statistic or have they noted what
>   the lecturer thought the statistic proved?
> 7. Do the notes use the lecturer's exact words or do they try to para-
>   phrase?

Listener 1's notes on lecture 2. 4

Purpose of university   DDM
                                                                     21 April

Variety of ⎰ • knowledge for its own sake ⟍   all
arg's: ⎱ • preserve culture   ⟩   true to
              • keep it pure   ⟩   some
              • pursuit of excellence   ⟋   extent
              • serve community

<u>Not</u> to preserve knowledge → library does this v. well

Bruner: library is [result] (?not cause?) of intell. act'vty

teach the <u>process</u> of 'knowledge-getting' (educ. reason
for university)

But: ALSO USEFUL.
Faculties are useful (agric, sc, tech)
Art useful - imbalance without (lack of aesthetic devel⁺.)

(If you don't study Art you
    may be a danger !!???)———— really??? ☹☹ !!!!

[qualifications]   [unemployment]

(the more)   (the less)

life expectancy 50 - 75   ⟨ Ed. level ⟩
              dev. developed ⟨ matters ⟩

Vice Chancellor   What's a degree for? ⟶
                                         (fact. kn.
                                           prob. solving
                                           gen. fluency
                                           numeracy
                                           pres. skills
                                           stamina)

Listener 2's notes on lecture 2. 4

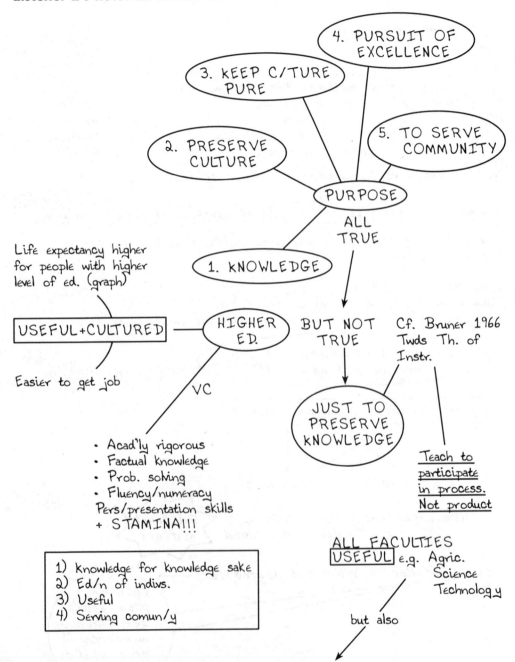

- *Well-organised notes will help you to retrieve the main ideas more efficiently.*
- *Always think about what you should copy down from an OHT.*

TASK 3

In another part of his lecture, the lecturer describes the differences between what is expected of undergraduates and other members of the university community.

3.1 Read the following set of expectations:

1. *will make an original contribution to knowledge*
2. *learns what others have said*
3. *adheres to taught rules*
4. *knows how to find out what other people have said*
5. *can evaluate the worth of new knowledge*

Which ones might apply to each of the following members of the university community?

(a) *students at the beginning of their university study*
(b) *master's students*
(c) *those involved in research*

3.2 Listen to the final extract and take notes. You should concentrate on understanding what the lecturer says about research and approaches to knowledge in the university.

You may like to try one of the methods of note-taking you saw in the two sets of notes in 2.4.

Review your notes, then compare what the lecturer said with *your* ideas in 3.1.

3.3 Write one or two more sentences to complete the following paragraph.

Different members of the university community are expected to have different approaches to knowledge and research ...

THE REFLECTIVE LEARNER

In this unit you have reflected on the importance of taking good notes, and you have looked at some of the criteria for effective notes. You have thought about how you can be sure you include the main ideas and important details in your notes, and you have had the chance to think about different note-taking styles that you might wish to use.

When you have a variety of note-taking styles available to you, and you understand what good notes should contain, you will feel more confident about taking notes in lectures.

Questions for your diary
1. How do you feel about your note-taking skills?
2. Do you have a favourite note-taking style? If so, why is it your favourite?
3. If you have discovered a new note-taking style in this unit, how will you get more practice in using it?

6 BUILDING MEANING AND SUMMARISING

In this unit you will:

- review your note-taking skills
- write summaries from notes
- think about building meaning from what you have understood

DISCUSSION

Thinking about building meaning and summarising

1. When you listen to a lecture in English now, how much can you understand?
2. What is a summary? How can writing a summary help you to know if you have understood a lecture?

TASK 1

1.1 Listen to a talk on vocabulary, given as part of a Study Skills programme for students preparing to study in English.

Take notes in your preferred way. When you have finished listening, spend two minutes checking your notes, filling in any gaps and making sure your notes are clear and sensible.

1.2 Use your notes to write a summary of the main ideas in the talk. Remember - a summary is not interested in *topic* (the subject of the talk). It is concerned with summarising the *argument* (what the speaker wants to say about the topic). Your summary should answer these three questions:

- *What is the speaker's view on the relationship between listening and reading vocabulary?*

- *What evidence does she offer to support this view?*
- *What advice does she offer?*

You should write between 80 and 120 words.

1.3   Compare your notes and summary with other students' notes and summaries. Have you all noted the same points and understood the talk in the same way? If not, try to work out why your notes and summaries are different.

TASK 2

2.1   Listen to an extract from a talk on the management of time and priorities, given in the same Study Skills programme. Take notes in your preferred style.

Spend two minutes silently reviewing your notes, checking that they are complete and make sense.

2.2   Use your notes to write a summary of the main ideas in the talk. This time, you should write between 120 and 150 words.

2.3   Compare your notes and summary with other students' notes and summaries.

Have you noted and summarised the same ideas? If not, why are they different?

> ## Soundbite
>
> - *A summary should be a clear and concise account of the important information.*

TASK 3

3.1   Until you are able to recognise most of what you hear, you will need to build meaning from what you are able to understand. This means that you will have to accept incomplete understanding. Sometimes you will have to speculate about what a lecturer means.

You are going to listen to an extract from the middle of a psychology lecture. You will hear the extract *only once*. Afterwards, you will need to complete the following statements:

1. *Students who listen to personal stereos while they write their essays are probably not ...*
2. *Glass and Singer discovered that if people ...*

Listen to the extract and make notes that will help you to recall the *overall meaning*.

3.2 Take two minutes to review your notes, then use what you have written to complete the statements in Task 3.1.

3.3 Check your statements with other students. How well do you think you understood the extract you heard in 3.1?

> ### Soundbite
>
> - *Willingness to accept some uncertainty is a very important characteristic of good listeners.*
> - *Good listeners do not 'switch off' when they do not understand everything – they do the best they can with what they have.*

TASK 4

4.1 You are going to hear an extract from a lecture on Trends in Society.

Read the following expressions used by the lecturer and try to predict what arguments he will present:

> *the sustainable use of the world's resources*
> *increasing urbanisation*
> *the rapid growth of technology*
> *a few predictions for the next century*
> *will be supported by evidence*
> *increasing political decentralisation*
> *increasing federalism*
> *radical economic restructuring*
> *a complex combination of social, economic and political factors*
> *major changes in the way the present system operates*
> *a progressive dissolution of larger units of production*
> *a growing simplification in lifestyle*
> *science will become simpler*

4.2 Now listen to the tape and take notes that will remind you of the lecturer's main arguments.

Spend two minutes reviewing your notes silently.

4.3 Look at the following statements. Use your notes to help you decide which ones the lecturer seems to believe are true.

1. *His predictions are likely to come true because they are short-term ones.*
2. *Economics and astronomy are less valid as sciences because their theories cannot be tested in the laboratory.*
3. *People will in the future move from large areas to smaller ones.*
4. *Capitalism will undergo a transformation which was not previously predicted.*
5. *The transformation experienced by capitalism will come about as a result of a global financial crash.*
6. *Our resources are too limited to allow everyone in the world to benefit from high technology so there will be a reversal of the trend towards it.*
7. *The scientific method will undergo a rigorous re-evaluation.*

4.4 Look at these descriptions of the lecturer's predictions. Which one(s) do you think best describe what you heard?

- *firmly founded in extensive research*
- *highly far-fetched*
- *impossible to judge*
- *likely to be true but difficult to support*
- *revealing an underlying bias*
- *quite sound*

4.5 Read the following extracts from some written articles. Which one do you think was written by the lecturer? In other words, which one expresses a similar point of view?

Extract A

It is impossible to make any sound prediction about major social changes that might occur in the twenty-first century. Twenty years ago, many of us might have voiced a different view – we could extrapolate and project with confidence. The uncertainty of the times has humbled us. We might with good reason suggest that life will tend to become simpler and technological advance will slow down. However, the reverse could equally be true.

Extract B

> A theory is scientific to the extent that it is possible to test it. In experimental science, it can be tested in the laboratory. With non-experimental science, we must wait until events produce the relevant evidence. Thus, it is inevitable that when a society becomes over-centralised, it reaches a stage when a reverse process begins to occur. This theory has been borne out by events in the 20th century and may reflect certain properties of the physical world.

Extract C

> One cannot rule out the possibility that an increasingly more sophisticated technological society will never come about. With the speed of innovation in the twentieth century, it was all too easy to assume that we would continue to improve our living standards with newer and better gadgets. However, certain social and economic changes may bring about a radical change in perspective with respect to what really constitutes a desirable lifestyle.

Extract D

> An economist is as unlikely to successfully predict a collapse in the system as a layperson. An infinite number of variables may come into play in an increasingly complex and uncertain world. In recent years, we have seen the credibility of economics as a scientific subject stretched to the limit. Very few of its theories can be tested, unlike, for example, physics or medicine, which are continually throwing up verifiable answers to unsolved questions as they probe ever deeper into the workings of the physical world.

4.6 Lecturers may sometimes use *idiomatic* expressions. They are quite common in spoken English, but you may not be familiar with many of them yet. They will not necessarily affect your ability to build meaning from what you hear.

Did you notice any idiomatic expressions in the extract you heard in 4.2? Do you think they affected your understanding of the lecturer's arguments?

THE REFLECTIVE LEARNER

In this unit you have reviewed your note-taking skills and reflected upon your understanding of what you hear. You have evaluated your ability to identify the important ideas through writing summaries from your notes. You have also seen the importance of being willing to build meaning, even when you are not sure that you have understood everything.

The ability to identify main ideas and a willingness to deal with uncertainty are both essential skills in academic listening.

Questions for your diary

1. If you think your note-taking needs to be more effective, what will you do to improve?
2. What strategies can you use to improve your understanding of information that is not clear to you?
3. Do you think that summary writing can help you to understand lectures better?

INTERLUDE 2

1 LEAPING TO CONCLUSIONS

TASK 1

1.1 Look at the title. What does *Leaping to conclusions* mean?

1. *Reading the first and last paragraphs and missing out the middle.*
2. *Not listening very carefully and then making the wrong decision.*
3. *Deciding something before you have all the necessary information.*
4. *Finishing something before you have had enough time to check it.*

1.2 When lecturers wish to introduce an idea, they often use an example. You're going to hear a lecturer using an example from his own experience.

Read these words and expressions from his example, and try to tell the story.

abroad
attending a conference
a health spa... attached to the main hotel
I wanted to use the swimming pool.
'You need a card,' she says.
'Do I need a towel?'
'You can get one at the pool.'
'You must pay,' he says.
I don't have any money.
I decided I wouldn't go for a swim.
'Why didn't you tell me that I had to pay?'
'Oh, there are so many things to tell the guests,' she says.

TASK 2

2.1 Now listen to the first extract. Decide if there are any differences between your story and what the lecturer describes in his example.

2.2 Listen to the second extract. Choose the correct statements from the following list:

1. *The speaker went to the dining room for breakfast.*
2. *He finished his breakfast within half an hour.*
3. *A woman he knew, called Julie, came into the dining room.*
4. *Julie was about to go for a swim.*
5. *He asked her if she had enjoyed her breakfast.*
6. *Julie started talking about the receptionist.*
7. *The receptionist had told her that she had to pay to use the pool.*
8. *The receptionist gave her a towel.*
9. *The receptionist didn't tell her that she needed a card.*
10. *Julie found a card when she got down to the pool.*

What was similar about the two people's experience of trying to go for a swim? What was different?

TASK 3

3.1 What do you think the lecturer might do in the next part of his talk?

1. *Give another example*
2. *Use the examples to introduce a main idea*
3. *Ask students to write about a similar thing that has happened to them*
4. *Summarise the points he has been trying to make so far*
5. *Finish his talk*

3.2 In the notes in 3.3, several words are abbreviated. Look at the list of abbreviations now and find them in the notes in 3.3.

Word	Abbreviation used
British	*Brit.*
expectations	*expects.*
receptionist	*recept.*
international	*int/l*
question	*qu.*
information	*info.*
communication	*comm.*
problem	*prob.*
generalisations	*general^{ns}*
observe	*obs.*
before	*b4*
swimming pool	*sw. pool*
premature conclusions	*prem. concls.*

3.3 Listen to the final extract and complete these notes:

Several thoughts:
1. A (1) _____ incident? (2 British/one local)
2. Expectations of Brit. guests - lots of (2) _____
   from receptionists.
3. Expects. of recept:
   (Hotel - int/l clientele - so why not all (3) _____ ?)
   Upbringing - only 1 qu. at a time? (Info by (4)_____?)
   Normal to have to (5) _____ to use a pool?

Comm. Failure
?? cultural or (6) _____
Illustrates: prob. of incidents → general/ns.
Need to obs. other (7) _____ and qu. (8) _____ .
i.e.: *** b4 diving into sw. pool, need to avoid 'leaping to
   prem concls.' ***

2 THE GREAT HUNGER

TASK 1

1.1   Look at the numbered areas on this map and identify the Republic of Ireland (which is also called Eire).

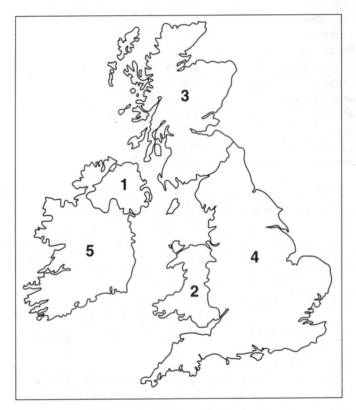

1.2   Read the following information and discuss the questions.

- *Until the 1920s, when it was divided, Ireland was a much bigger country than it is now, and it was part of the United Kingdom.*

Look at the map again and identify the areas which remained part of the United Kingdom after the division.

- *The division took place because the majority of Irish people (who were Catholic Christians) did not want their country to be governed by the English (most of whom were Protestant Christians).*

Do you think everyone was happy about the division?

  • *During the nineteenth century, thousands of Irish people emigrated.*

Where do you think most of them went?

1.3 In the late 1840s, there was a huge problem in Ireland. Look at these expressions, and decide what the problem was, and what happened:

> *dependent on the potato*
> *invaded by a kind of fungus*
> *destroyed the potatoes*
> *died of starvation*
> *couldn't pay the rent*
> *evict the people*
> *destroying the cottages*
> *1½ million people emigrated*

1.4 Even in recent times, some people in Northern Ireland have continued to fight for independence from Britain, and many Americans have sent money to support them. Why do you think Americans have supported this fight?

TASK 2

2.1 Read each expression and choose the best meaning:

1. *the population was very vulnerable*
   (a) the people were at risk
   (b) the people had a lot of problems

2. *forcing the people to become more industrialised*
   (a) trying to make people leave the land and work in factories
   (b) making people join groups fighting for better working conditions

3. *people were not particularly sympathetic*
   (a) people didn't have much information
   (b) people were not very concerned

4. *extremely meaningless work*
   (a) work that people do not understand
   (b) work with no purpose

5. *at the height of [the problem]*
   (a) when [the problem] was solved
   (b) when [the problem] was worst

6. *they didn't want the population to become too dependent on these soup kitchens*
   (a) people were discouraged from relying on the soup kitchens
   (b) people were told not to use the soup kitchens

7. *these attempts met with only very limited success*
   (a) they were not very successful
   (b) they did not try to achieve very much

8. *many died en route*
   (a) many people died at the end of their journey
   (b) many people died before they finished their journey

2.2   What do the following words and expressions mean?

it has been coloured by a number of events
completely inedible
the cumulative effect
absentee landlords
absolutely destitute
grain
demoralising
they set up soup kitchens
famine
convert
workhouses
oppressors

TASK 3

3.1   Listen to the first extract and answer these questions:

1. *What was the population of Ireland in 1845?*
2. *How did the people who didn't own land manage to grow their potatoes?*
3. *What did a working man eat for dinner?*
4. *Why did the potato crop fail?*
5. *Apart from hunger, what other problems did the Irish have in 1846-1847?*

3.2   Listen to the second extract and answer these questions:

> 6. *What did some landlords try to do to help their tenants?*
> 7. *Why didn't all the landlords try to help?*

3.3   Listen to the third extract and answer this question:

> 8. *What four reasons does the speaker give for the lack of sympathy shown by the British government and people?*

3.4   Listen to the fourth extract and answer this question:

> 9. *The speaker mentions four ways in which help was given to the Irish. What are these four ways?*

3.5   Listen to the final extract and answer this question:

> 10. *What did the Irish themselves do to stop themselves from starving to death?*

UNIT

7

KEY IDEAS

In this unit you will:

- practise identifying the main points a lecturer wants to make
- use summary techniques to check that you understand each part of a lecture

DISCUSSION

Thinking about key ideas

1. Why is it important to recognise key ideas (or main points) in a lecture?
2. Why do lecturers use examples?
3. How do you know that you have not lost the main thread of a lecturer's argument?

TASK 1

1.1 You are going to listen to extracts from a lecture on food in Britain by Professor H.E. Nursten, an authority on food science. (Prof. Nursten says he is interested in all aspects of food, having eaten it all his life!)

First, look at this OHT which Professor Nursten used to help the listeners to follow the structure of this part of his lecture.

What do you think he might say about each of these headings?

Professor H.E. Nursten

> **Food in Britain**
>
> - **Introduction: choice of food**
> - **Cultural and historical influences on eating patterns: geography, population and climate**
> - **Trade in food**

1.2 Choose a suitable note-taking style. Listen to the introduction to Prof Nursten's lecture and take notes of the main point(s) he is making, plus any information which helps you to understand those ideas.

1.3 Look at your notes and review them silently for two minutes. Then identify ideas that you would include in a brief summary.

Plan an outline for your summary.

1.4 Now compare your summary outline with the suggested outline on page 61. If you have any ideas in your outline which are not included in the page 61 outline, why did you think they were important when you heard them?

1.5 Discuss the following questions.

> 1. What is the key idea that the lecturer was presenting to his listeners?
> 2. What is the relationship between the key idea and the four factors in our choice of food?
> 3. Where does this idea occur in the plan for the summary on page 61? Where did it occur in the extract?
> 4. Why does the lecturer end his introduction by talking about what the *British* eat?

TASK 2

2.1 Look at the OHT in 1.1. What is Professor Nursten going to talk about next? How will you continue your notes from 1.2?

Listen to the second extract and take notes that show any arguments and relationships that you think are important.

2.2 After you have reviewed your notes, use them to discuss the following questions:

> 1. What were the key ideas that the lecturer wanted listeners to understand?
> 2. How did the lecturer make sure the listeners understood these ideas?
> 3. Are all your group's notes clear and well-organised? Do they all contain the same points? If anyone noted any examples, are they useful examples to remember?
> 4. If you have any ideas in your notes which are different from others in your group, why did you think it was important to note them down?

TASK 3

3.1 Look back at your notes from 2.1 and think about what Professor Nursten has been discussing.

He has just indicated that he wants to talk 'a bit more about the population'. What do you think the next key idea will be? Why?

3.2 Look at the following transcript of the first part of the third extract.

Can you find the key idea you have just predicted? If not, what do you now think the key idea is?

How does the lecturer signal that he is stating the key idea?

> Well, as soon as you think about population, you obviously need to think about the area of the country in relation to the population. Well, the current population is about sixty million. And it has been steady for quite a while in spite of the traffic I've talked about, both outwards and inwards. Sixty million people are living in this country, and the important thing to appreciate, is that we can't feed sixty million people

5

> with the amount of food which we grow here. That's very important. Clearly we have to import some extra food.

3.3 On the OHT in 1.1, the lecturer mentioned *Trade*. What key idea do you think he will discuss next? Can you find this idea in the transcript of the next part of the third extract, below? Which words does he use to make sure the students notice this key idea?

> And so our trade in food is a most important consideration, and that's why I've put these figures up on the board. Well, it takes a bit of time to just have a look, er, at those figures. Perhaps the best thing to do is to look at the total at the bottom. Well, you can see from those figures, that we export only about half as much as we import, so the balance of   5
> trade is very much, in terms of food, is very much, er, against this country. But the interesting thing, I think, is that there's such a big trade in food. If we don't grow enough food in this country to feed ourselves, it's surprising that we should export as much as we do.

3.4 In the next part of the third extract, the lecturer refers to the following figures, which he has put on an OHT. Look at the two TOTAL figures.

TRADE IN FOODSTUFFS £m (rounded)	Exports	Imports
Meat and meat preparations	1080	2600
Dairy products and eggs	740	1210
Fish	755	1230
Cereals and cereal preparations	1590	1140
Vegetables and fruit	470	4300
Sugar and sugar preparations and honey	420	890
Coffee, tea, cocoa, spices etc.	680	1280
Other	1265	1960
TOTAL	7000	14610

Now listen to the complete extract and continue your notes. Focus particularly on the key idea you identified in 3.3, and on information which supports that idea.

3.5   After you have reviewed your notes, share them with other students and see if you have all identified similar supporting ideas.

> ### Soundbite
>
> • *Remember to keep relating your understanding to the key ideas as you continue listening.*

TASK 4

4.1   Look at the *Trade in Foodstuffs* OHT from 3.4 again, and also look at these phrases which Professor Nursten uses:

> *you can see what the trade in food looks like...*
> *you can see that meat and meat preparations...*
> *whereas in dairy products ...*
> *fish, again, we import considerably more than...*
> *for cereals, we do actually export...*
> *tropical fruits, well quite obviously...*
> *cane is a tropical crop...*

What do you think he is going to do in the extract? Will you take notes? Why or why not?

4.2   Listen to the final extract. You will need to keep looking at the *Trade in Foodstuffs* OHT.

If you take notes, try to show how the information you hear is connected to the key ideas you have already noted.

4.3   Look back over all your notes, and summarise what you have learned about food in Britain. A written summary of this information should not be longer than 200 words.

THE REFLECTIVE LEARNER

In this unit you have had more practice in identifying the key ideas in a lecture. You've seen how (a) summarising each part of a lecture, and (b) predicting what will come next, can help you to make sure you are following the argument.

When you listen to your lectures, you probably won't be able to write summaries during the lecture. But you can remember to keep checking that your growing understanding makes sense, and that your comprehension has not gone 'off track'. Mentally summarising and predicting as you listen will also help you to keep concentrating.

Questions for your diary
1. When you are listening, how will you make sure that the ideas you have noted down are the key ideas?
2. What opportunities can you find at the moment to practise summarising and predicting?

SUMMARY OUTLINE FOR TASK 1.4

People/ food – complex relationship. Four interrelated factors:
- availability
- affordability
- wholesomeness
- enjoyment

UNIT 8

PRIOR KNOWLEDGE

In this unit you will:

- learn about 'prior knowledge'
- discover what it is like to listen both with and without prior knowledge
- investigate whether what you have read about a topic affects your note-taking

DISCUSSION

Thinking about prior knowledge

1. What do you think 'prior knowledge' means?
2. What sort of prior knowledge might be relevant when you listen to a lecture?
3. How could prior knowledge be dangerous?

TASK 1

1.1 Cover the words in 1.2 before you do this task.

Listen to the tape and take notes of the speaker's main points. What was the lecturer talking about? Would you be able to write a summary from your notes?

1.2 Look at the following made-up 'words' and phrases which you heard on the tape. Notice that the words are 'fun words' — they are not real English words!

Spend a few minutes learning their 'meaning'.

Word or phrase	Meaning
dingleness	*boldness; aggressiveness in the marketplace*
gabbability	*flexibility*
the hegical forms of control	*the traditional restrictions on employees' freedom to make decisions*
moobling permilts	*newly-developed financial markets*
a shinger	*a coward*
his stogglement on developments	*his influence on what happened*
trantable for	*responsible for*

1.3 Listen to the tape again and add to your notes from 1.1.

1.4 Review your notes, then compare your second set of notes with the notes you took in 1.1. Was it easier to take notes when you knew more of the vocabulary?

> ## Soundbite
>
> • *If you do not know the concepts or the vocabulary, listening will be more difficult.*

TASK 2

2.1 You're now going to try out this idea of prior knowledge with real words and a real lecture. The two extracts you will hear come from an education lecture. The topic is *Learning and remembering*.

Read the following phrases. Discuss their meaning and what they suggest the lecturer will talk about.

the concept of attention
like a torch
part of short-term memory
think about the metaphor
focusing on things and ignoring other things
hearing and not hearing
you're processing what you're focusing on
what is ignored is not processed
this is where the second theory comes in
theories ... about how memory is used in general
fundamental distinction between ... long-term and ... short-term memory
you're mentally repeating the number in ... short-term memory

> *short-term memory is the active part of long-term memory*
> *within short-term memory, you have attention*
> *three concentric circles*
> *attention ... is the part of short-term memory that is in focus*

2.2 The extract deals with *two* theories of attention. What does this suggest to you about a suitable note-taking style?

Now listen to the extract and take notes. Do not look at the phrases in 2.1 while you are listening.

2.3 Review your notes, then compare them with other students' notes.

Did the pre-listening discussion of vocabulary and ideas help you to understand and take good notes?

2.4 Identify the main ideas from your notes and write a five or six sentence summary of what you heard.

2.5 Look at these phrases which you will hear in the next part of the lecture. Discuss their meaning and the ideas that they suggest to you.

> *psychological experiment*
> *two different groups were asked to read the text*
> *the house-buyer group*
> *the second group*
> *this house might be one that you could burgle*
> *afterwards they were given a recall activity*
> *they were asked to remember everything they could*
> *concentrated on information that might be useful to house buyers*
> *the state of the roof*
> *concentrated on things that were useful to burglars*
> *the type of security arrangements*
> *there was a second recall task*
> *the groups were asked to switch perspectives*
> *came up with some more details*

Listen to the next section of the tape and continue your notes.

2.6 Review your notes, then identify the main ideas from your *complete* set of notes and write a summary of what the lecturer said.

Did the pre-listening discussion of vocabulary and ideas help you to understand, complete your notes satisfactorily and write an accurate summary?

Task 3

3.1 Read either Text 1 (on page 66) or Text 2 (on page 67). Make sure you understand the vocabulary.

3.2 Discuss what you have understood with others who have read the same text.

3.3 Listen to the tape and note down what you think are the important ideas and information.

3.4 Review your notes, then compare them with those of someone who read a different text from you and discuss the following questions:

- *Have you recorded the same main ideas?*
- *Do you think your notes and your understanding of the extract were affected by the reading you did before you listened? If so, how?*

Soundbite

- *Your understanding of a lecture may be affected by what you expect to hear.*

THE REFLECTIVE LEARNER

In this unit you have evaluated the effect of prior knowledge, both of vocabulary and of content, on your understanding. You have also been able to see whether information you have read before a lecture changes what you write in your notes.

When you listen to a lecture, you will find it easier to understand what you hear if you have done some reading beforehand.

Questions for your diary
1. What will you do to make sure that you have maximum prior knowledge before attending a lecture?
2. What opportunities can you find at the moment to practise reading and then listening to a lecture?
3. Apart from reading, how else can you prepare to listen to a lecture?

TASK 3.1 — TEXT 1

Aristotle and Newton

A major early figure in the history of science was Aristotle, a Greek
philosopher who lived in the 4th century B.C. About two thousand years
later, Isaac Newton (1642-1727) conceived his influential scientific ideas
in England. Both Aristotle and Newton developed theories to explain the
nature of motion and matter.   5

Aristotle believed that the natural state of bodies was one of rest.
According to his theory, a material object would remain at rest unless an
external force acted to move it. He thought that everything in the universe
had its natural place and this meant remaining in one place. Newton, on
the other hand, believed that the natural state was one of motion and that   10
any material object would move unless something acted on it to stop it.
He thought that a state of rest was not the natural one — rather, it was to
be perceived as an exception to the general rule about material objects
always being in a state of motion.

Aristotle's idea seemed to be based on common sense but Newton showed   15
that we cannot claim that science is only what T.H. Huxley, writing in the
latter half of the 19th century, called 'trained and organised common
sense'. If that is all it is, then Aristotle's common-sense idea would have
been right, and Newton would have been wrong. But our present scientific
understanding leads us to believe that Newton's first law of motion   20
describes the world more accurately. Far from any comfortable notion of
being able to explain any laws of nature through the application of
common sense, Newton apparently claimed he felt like a small child
playing with pebbles on the shores of a vast sea of knowledge.

Task 3.1 — Text 2

Thomas Kuhn

Thomas Kuhn was a 20th century philosopher of science who was very influential in changing the way people think about science. Most people are probably familiar with the term 'paradigm shift', but they may not know that it was Kuhn who invented the term. Kuhn defined a scientific paradigm as a 'constellation of achievements – concepts, values, techniques   5 etc. — shared by a scientific community and used by that community to define legitimate problems and solutions' (Kuhn 1962). At any one time, science was seen as operating within commonly agreed norms of practice and social acceptability. For example, there was a dramatic change in the concepts and ideas of physics in the early part of the 20th century. The   10 mechanistic views of Descartes and Newton were challenged by revelations about the sub-atomic world. The old concepts and methods of science were inadequate to explain these new phenomena. This required a change in thinking, described by Kuhn as a 'paradigm shift', which did not mean a complete dismissal of everything that had come before but, rather, a   15 progression.

Kuhn suggested that scientists operate within current paradigms, which may be influenced by social, religious or moral factors. While science, in his view, was not arbitrary in its development, scientists do not stand entirely outside the society to which they belong. Thus, the paradigm shift   20 which led to the emergence of quantum physics may be viewed in the light of a broad climate of cultural uncertainty in the first decades of the 20th century.

Kuhn's theory created an enormous amount of controversy and debate. In fact, as well as being the most frequently cited academic book of recent   25 decades, *The Structure of Scientific Revolutions* may well go down in history as the most misunderstood one of the 20th century.

UNIT 9

REVIEW

In this unit you will:

- evaluate the progress you have made in listening and note-taking
- identify any areas of listening you need to keep working on

DISCUSSION

Reviewing your progress

1. What styles of note-taking do you now use? Do you use abbreviations and symbols?
2. Can you now recognise the main ideas and examples? How do you highlight them in your notes or on handouts?
3. Is it easier to listen to a lecture on a topic you are familiar with?
4. Do you think you know enough words to understand lectures in your subject?
5. If you still find it hard to understand what you hear, what do you think is causing this problem?

TASK 1

1.1 In Unit 8 you looked at the idea that if you know something about the topic or are familiar with the vocabulary, it will probably be easier to understand a lecture.

You are going to listen to a lecture about water and agriculture, given by Professor M. J. Rolls, of the University of Reading, U.K. He is an expert on establishing and managing information systems to support the introduction of innovative technologies into agricultural communities.

Professor Rolls discussing crops and water in Romania.

To prepare for the lecture, read the following article. Make notes on the main ideas and examples.

Take Two of Hydrogen and One of Oxygen

The need to feed a growing population is putting a strain on the world's supply of our most precious commodity: water.

With 97% of the world's water too salty to be drunk or used in agriculture, the global supply of this most essential commodity is in need of very careful management. Although the idea of a shortage in the world's water no doubt seems strange to someone fortunate enough to live in a relatively high-rainfall country such as Canada or New Zealand, the fact is that 40% of the world's population experiences constant or occasional water shortages.

Although dams can be built to store water for use in dry regions and dry seasons, thus evening out distribution through space and time, the costs of redistribution are very high. Not only is there the cost of the engineering itself, but there is also an environmental cost to be considered. Where valleys are flooded to create dams, communities are lost and wildlife habitats destroyed. Furthermore, water may flow easily through pipes, but it cannot be transported from one side of the world to the other. Each country must therefore look to the management of its own water resources to supply its own requirements.

This is particularly troubling for countries with established or developing agricultural industries in irrigation-dependent areas. In Texas, where farmers are heavily involved in beef production, the over-use of irrigation water from the Ogallala aquifer* has resulted in a 25% depletion of the water stores. In the Central Valley area of south-western USA, a huge subsidised water engineering project provided water for farming in dry valleys, but much of the water use has been poorly-managed.

Saudi Arabia's attempts to grow wheat in desert areas has seen the pumping of huge quantities of irrigation water from underground reserves. Because there is no rainfall in these areas, such reserves are not restocked, and it is estimated that fifty years of pumping will see them run dry.

But it is not just agriculture that depletes a country's water resources. Increasing urbanisation brings in its wake heavy demands on water supplies. In cities such as Bangkok, Mexico City and Beijing, these demands have caused water tables to drain faster than rainfall can replenish them.

Even when water is available, it may not always be drinkable. Poor water management results in poor quality water, with micro-organisms threatening the health of the population. Pollution too is a major concern, with recent history providing some spectacular examples of contamination from industrial products or accidents.

With water such a vital resource for the world, it is perhaps not surprising that much time, effort and money goes into research associated with its use, conservation and quality.

*a water-bearing layer in rock or soil

1.2   In class, compare your notes on the text with other students' notes.

TASK 2

2.1   Now listen to Professor Roll's lecture and take notes, using the method that
works best for you. Remember to note the *topic* and *structure* of the lecture as
outlined in the introduction. Listening to how the lecturer limits the scope of the
lecture will help you to identify the topic. Also remember to note any important
points that he makes in the conclusion.

When you finish your notes, review them very carefully. Try to make sure you
have written down everything you think is important. Highlight anything that
you think will help you, and check that connections between ideas are clear.
Check that you have put the *title, the lecturer's name* and *the date.*

*Back in an
academic
environment,
Professor Rolls
gives a lecture to
students.*

2.2   Look at the introduction and the conclusion to Professor Roll's lecture in the
transcript at the end of the book (pages 121 and 125), and compare these with
your notes.

Did you note down the correct topic and structure? Did you note down the
point that the lecturer made in the conclusion?

2.3   Look at Section 1 of the transcript (page 122). Highlight the main ideas and any other important information in this section.

Compare what you have highlighted in the transcript with what you actually wrote in your notes. Make any changes to this part of your notes that you think will improve them.

2.4   Look at Section 2 of the transcript (page 123) and highlight the main ideas and information as you did with Section 1.

Compare what you have highlighted in the transcript with what you actually wrote in your notes, and make any changes that will improve your notes.

2.5   Now do the same with Section 3.

2.6   Look at the two sets of notes on pages 73 to 75. Discuss with other students any differences in *content* and *organisation* between these notes and your 'improved' notes.

TASK 3

3.1   Listen to the lecture again. This time, read the transcript while you listen.

Identify any *information* and any *words* which you know you didn't understand when you heard the lecture the first time.

3.2   Look back at your notes, and find what you originally wrote down when you heard the words or sections of the lecture which you have just identified.

Think about the reason you didn't understand some items, and classify each item that you did not understand as follows:

1.   *I didn't know the word or expression.*
2.   *I knew the word in its written form but I didn't recognise it when I heard it.*
3.   *I didn't understand this because the words were linked together.*
4.   *I didn't understand this because I was still trying to understand the previous part.*
5.   *I didn't realise that this part was important.*
6.   *I lost concentration or interest.*
7.   *Other reasons.*

3.3   Identify which classification or classifications you have used most often.

If you seem to have a problem in one or two particular areas, what can you continue to do about these problems after you have finished this book?

3.4   You have now reached the end of the book.

Look at The Reflective Learner box below. Read the questions and answer them for yourself. Then share your answers with other students.

THE REFLECTIVE LEARNER

1. Using a 1 – 5 scale (1 = poor or low; 5 = very good or very high), give yourself a score on your progress in the following aspects of listening and be prepared to justify your choice:
   (a) decoding normal spoken English
   (b) coping with speed and different accents
   (c) recognising the structure of a lecture
   (d) identifying key ideas
   (e) taking notes
   (f) summarising from your notes
   (g) listening, looking at an OHT and taking notes
   (h) sustaining attention
   (i) feeling confident about listening to lectures in your subject
2. In which area have you made the most progress since the beginning of this course? What helped you to make progress?
3. In which area do you want to make further progress? What will you do to achieve that?
4. Do you intend to record your lectures? If so, how will you use the recordings?
5. Do you plan to co-operate with other students to make your listening easier? If so, what will you do?
6. What sources of continuing help are available to you while you are studying your own subject?

For your diary
You can write about any of the above questions if you wish.

UNIT 9: 2.6

Notes 1

WATER   Prof. Rolls
                                   12 October

A.   3 characteristics

Exists as (1)   solid 80% 'refrigerated' in poles!
         (2)   gas – heat regulator for whole globe thru
                     evaporation from oceans
         (3)   liquid 97% salty

B.   It cycles   transfers between 3 forms
              earth → cloud
     500BC thought ↑   → rain ↓↓
              sea forces up thru earth

     total amount – finite   1m. deep layer circulates p.a.

C.   Things dissolve in it
              – collects salts from soil
              – carries particles suspended imp. for deltas

FARMS

     irrig. sys. 4000BC
water –   clean not necessary
     only needed growth period

a) ancient   – land fallow 1 yr.
             crops – 2yrs. supply

b) irrigation –   make channels
                  keep clear
                  share use

  work   small groups self-reliant users
       a) local   b) national level

FARMING

Types water: 1) surface   – sky
           2) ground   – fallen + stored
              Effective use – double crop prod.

<u>But</u> rain   erosion (explosion on falling)

      health risk – more snails and insects!
      soil damage from salt left
      disputes: who will have how much when??

2 issues

①   better | retention |

      good cover plants
      barriers
      high organic matter – retain
      find 'suitable' crops
      manipulate planting time
irrig. methods – watering-can to trickle system

②   way of | obtaining | by plant

      a) roots chasing – rainfall simultaneous with
                      planting – wet season beg.

      b) water upwards from 'reservoir' supply – hope
                  it lasts till mature

<u>CONCLUSION</u>
- Farm production not adequately adjusted to irrigation
- Irrigation practice not adj'd to environment

Needs to be <u>managed</u>

UNIT 9: 2.6

Notes 2

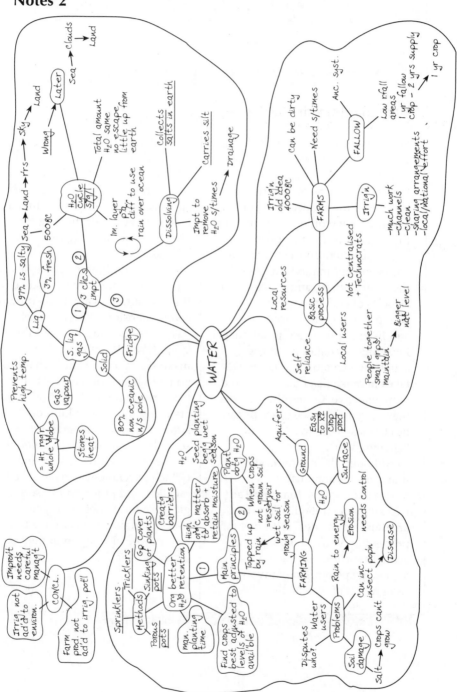

EXTRA RESOURCES FOR UNIT 1, TASK 3.1

S for Strategy, V for Victory

Winning the war the Greek way

When the Ancient Greeks went to war, they depended on what they called *strategia*, or the art of war. If their *strategia* was ineffective, they had very little chance of winning, because they would not be making the best use of their resources.

It is such a useful word that it has been kept in modern English in the form *strategy*, and it is used in all sorts of endeavours such as war, politics, finance, romance - and listening in a second language. Listening strategies are those actions which a user of language takes to make listening easier and more effective. Or in other words, they are what listeners do (or can do) to make sure they win the 'listening war'.

Although the matter is still under discussion, many researchers believe that there are two kinds of strategies. The first are those which deal with mental processing, with the business of actually sorting out the words that are being spoken. They involve recognition of words, the 'unpacking' of meaning from a text, and storing and remembering what has been heard. They are sometimes known as *direct strategies*, because they operate directly on the language of the text; they are what you do with the words you hear.

The second kind of strategies are those involved when listeners think about, or evaluate their own comprehension. When you ask, 'What else do I know about this subject?' or 'What can I do to make sure I understand what I'm going to hear?' or 'Am I satisfied that I really understand this?' you are using the second kind of strategy. These strategies are sometimes called *indirect strategies*.

These two kinds of strategies (which psychologists have called *cognitive* and *metacognitive* strategies) are fundamental to what a user of language does. They can be a powerful weapon in the listening war.

EXTRA RESOURCES FOR
UNIT 4, TASK 4.2

Here are twenty more signpost expressions. Can you classify them according to the categories given on page 31?

1. *That's all I want to say about X.*
2. *Can anyone think of an example of this?*
3. *This is not the only way of looking at it, and perhaps not even the best way.*
4. *Anyone got any ideas?*
5. *A case in point was the collapse of Barings.*
6. *I'd like to come back to that in a moment.*
7. *This seems to be the most satisfactory explanation.*
8. *So that's the essence of the theory put forward by X.*
9. *To get back to the main point, which is the effect of this merger on the other US car manufacturers.*
10. *At this point I'd like to say something about X's conclusions.*
11. *So, let's take a closer look at why this theory fails to account for the phenomena.*
12. *That, then, is another way of looking at the same problem.*
13. *So, in effect, this appears to be the better method.*
14. *Can you think of any instances of this?*
15. *This outcome is a very important one.*
16. *Take the case of the plantain in Africa.*
17. *So that's a very good example of the first kind of problem.*
18. *What I propose to do next is to look at this whole issue from a historical perspective.*
19. *Brooke's theory seems the more plausible one.*
20. *You'll remember the flaws we found in X's research.*

TRANSCRIPTS OF TAPES

UNIT 1, TASK 2.2

Interview with Tulay Balci (6′54″)

Interviewer: Tulay, you're doing a PhD in Dairy Science aren't you?

Tulay: That's right.

Interviewer: And before you did the PhD, I know that you did a Master's degree, Master of Science, wasn't it?

Tulay: Yes, Master of Science in Dairy Science.   5

Interviewer: So that would have meant that you had a lot of lectures?

Tulay: We had a lot of lectures, yes, like twenty f... hours of lectures in a week.

Interviewer: That must have been very tiring, to do twenty hours of lectures. Was it?

Tulay: Yeah, that was very tiring. Er, apart from the ones we slept.   10

Interviewer: You slept?

Tulay: Well, I wouldn't say I sl... quite slept, but I was just about to.

Interviewer: I'm surprised you admit that you were going to sleep in lectures. Why was that?

Tulay: Er, I thought some of the lecturers, er, kept the lecture boring, er, by not   15
changing their voices or b... by, by not changing the subject, you know, kept
on talking at the same subject all t... all the time, for fifty minutes, say.

Interviewer: Did you find that many of the lectures were about subjects that you
were already familiar with?

Tulay: Yeah, I found that, because my first degree was dairy sciences one, so I   20
didn't have any problem with getting familiar with the subject, or...

Interviewer: So you were able to understand the content of the subject, because
you were familiar, or the content of the lecture, because you were familiar
already with it?

Tulay: Yeah, w... with most of them, yeah.   25

Interviewer: You would find that an advantage then.

Tulay: Yeah, I, definitely. There, there is an advantage, yes.

Interviewer: What about the, the subjects on your course that you were not so
familiar with? What did you do to prepare yourself for those lectures?

Tulay: The thing is, I... lecturers make you easier... make, make it easier for you,   30
because they would give handouts at the beginning of each term, or each
lecture, for you to read beforehand, or er, even, even for example, i... if you
don't know the words, some terms, you would see it on the handout and get
familiar with them. You may be able to use a dictionary beforehand, if you go
home and study.   35
Interviewer: Could you describe a typical handout that you were given, at the
beginning of term for instance?
Tulay: Er, they weren't big texts. They were just, er, about the main points of the
subject, what he was going to say, and the titles, er, and the further reading.
Er, they would give you the titles, and a reference list, and you would go to   40
the library and, er, according to the titles, choose, choose a book and just read
about it, before and, or after that.
Interviewer: So you were given plenty of warning, erm, in order to help you
prepare for the lecture [Yes]. What about the handouts that were given to you
at the beginning of the lecture? They would be much more focused, presum-   45
ably, were they, on the lecture for that particular day? Could, could you
describe a typical handout given on the day of the lecture?
Tulay: For example, we had a nutrition lecture, and it had, er, some pictures,
some very small, er, titles. She just, er, our lecturer just talked about it. So, I
wouldn't say you, you have t... you take the handout and read, read about it   50
and understand something. You just have to have it with the lecture, so it
wouldn't, even, er, s... some of them wouldn't, er, have helped if you had it
beforehand. But some of d..., some of did, yeah.
Interviewer: Did you use the handouts during class at all, for instance for note-
taking?   55
Tulay: I did, yeah. Most of the time I didn't have to use a big note-book to take
my notes. I just take some little words, you know, little notes onto the
handout itself.
Interviewer: Apart from finding some of the lectures boring, and falling asleep
[laughter], which I hope you've never told your lecturers, by the way, [No, I   60
didn't.] did you have any other problems with listening to your lectures?
Tulay: Erm, s..., er, most of them are quite all right, but one of our lecturers did
have, did have a quiet voice, and he used a microphone because we were
having the lecture with a, in a big classroom, so there were a lot of people, so
he did use a, use a microphone for us to be able to understand him and, lis...   65
er, fo..., erm, you know listen to him better [And to follow what he says], hear
him, yes, follow what he was saying [Yes, yes].
Interviewer: After the lecture, did the students get together at all, in, in small
groups or just informally, to discuss the content of the lecture?
Tulay: Erm, not about the lectures. I've, I remember that we did it about the   70
practical work, like the lab work, and the lab reports we had to write. But not
about the lecture. I don't remember, er, talking to anyone about the lecture.
Interviewer: Do you know if any other students did that at all?
Tulay: Yeah, there, there were quite, er, you know small groups, one or three, one

or two, small groups that, they must have done that. Er, actually, er, what a   75
m... what my experience is that, after my MSc you know, I went on to the
PhD and, er, actually gave some practical classes to the MSc students, and I
saw that they were, they had a big group and worked together all the time,
and I thought it was very nice. I... in our class we didn't have that, but s... in
some of the classes they helped each other.   80

Interviewer: If you were going to give advice to somebody now on, erm, listening
to lectures, is there any one thing you can think of that y... that might have
helped you more with your lectures?

Tulay: Er, I would say, if you are given the handouts, and the reference lists, er,
just go and get familiar with the subject before you go on to the lecture. It will   85
definitely make it, erm, much easier for you to understand and follow the
lecture, even if w..., no matter how he is, how boring he is, or she is, I don't
know. Mm.

Interviewer: So this question of lecturers being boring is obviously still a big thing
in your memory. [Yeah, it is.] What about the more entertaining lecturers?   90
Let's have a look at some of the more positive sides [*laughter*]. What did, erm,
the good lecturers do, to make you feel that these were good lectures and that
you were enjoying them?

Tulay: For example, he would start a lecture with a joke, so it will cheer you up
in nine o'clock in the morning, on Monday morning especially, and then he   95
would, er, talk about the subject, and in the middle of a very boring thing, he
would say a joke, and then, or he would talk about his previous experience
and you would admire him, even more, and it would make it more attractive,
you to the subject, er, and then you will think that in twenty years time, I will
be one of, you know, one of the lecturers like this, and I will be telling all my   100
experience to my students. That's what I felt.

UNIT 1, TASK 3.1

Listening strategies (3'12")

Hello everyone. Now I know you've been thinking about listening strategies, er,
so I thought I'd talk to you today about strategies and what exactly they are, so
that perhaps you can then relate what I've said to the listening process, and it can
help you.

First of all I think we need to look at this word *strategy* and ask ourselves, where   5
does it come from, and what does it mean? The Ancient Greeks used the word
strategia, erm, and they used strategies to help them to win wars. In other words,
they thought about what resources they had, and then they thought about how
they could use those resources best, in order to be victorious against their
enemies.   10

In the modern world today, people still use strategies, for example erm, politicians use strategies to win elections, and businessmen use strategies in order to close business deals successfully. What sort of strategies can you use for listening? How can you use the resources you have best, to make you successful at listening? 15

Psychologists seem to think that there are two kinds of strategies. There are strategies which are to do with mental processing. For example, erm, they're to do with recognising the words you hear, they're to do with understanding the meaning of words, even when perhaps you don't know the meaning of each single word in a sentence or a phrase, but you still manage to understand the 20 meaning of what you've heard. They're even to do with remembering what you've heard, and making sense of it so that you can understand what you're actually hearing now. These are direct strategies. They're what you do with the words that you actually hear.

The other kind of strategy is rather more indirect. It's to do with evaluating your 25 comprehension, erm evaluating what you've heard, er, and erm, it's to do with evaluating the, y..., your ability to actually comprehend. So you may ask yourself er, how can I help myself to understand more? How much have I understood of what I've, er, been listening to? And, what do I know about the subject, that will help me to understand better? These two different kinds of strategies are called 30 *cognitive* and *metacognitive* strategies by psychologists. It doesn't matter if you can't remember what they're called. The important thing is to remember that there are strategies, there are resources which you can use effectively to help you to listen, to help you to understand what you've heard. As you become aware of these strategies, you should find that your ability to listen and understand 35 improves.

Unit 2, Task 1.3

Sentences from lectures and seminars (0'6")

1. These early examples of the art are now highly sought after.
2. Advice is available on the provision of handrails and ramps.
3. Some commentators say the damage generated by his divorce was under-estimated.
4. We need to develop policies supporting the economic independence of 5 women.

Unit 2, Task 3.1

Language use in society (1'52")

Right, O.K. Erm, now, it's, erm, often said that when two English people meet, they learn a lot about each other just by opening their mouths, and uttering a

few words, I mean just a sentence even. Erm, so for example, let's think, people on a train, in a railway carriage. Let's imagine one's asking the other to open the window, well, or maybe close the window, perhaps that's a, a more normal   5
situation. Now, there's no neutral way of doing this, so in asking, one is, always, revealing something about oneself.

You can ask in different ways, can't you? 'Could you possibly close the window please? It's a bit cold in here.' 'Oi, shut the window.' Now obviously, first of all, one's attitude to the other person is shown here. Now that might be deliberate.   10
One form is more polite, the other's less polite. Another point is that pronunciation shows one's regional origin. So, for example, we have Scottish, northern, London, and other accents.

All of this, that I've talked about so far, can be found in other countries and with other languages, so that people can be polite, or impolite, people's accents reveal   15
where they come from.

But in England we've got something else. Let's listen again. 'Could you possibly close the window please. I..., it's a bit cold in here.' 'Oi, close the window!' The first is BBC English, more or less, the second, cockney, or something similar. What do these show? Well these show social class. So as well as regional origin,   20
one is showing one's social class.

UNIT 2, TASK 3.2

Language use in society (1'37″)

Right, let's take the situation where we have, say, erm an American, a German and a Japanese in the railway carriage, and they are being asked to close the window. Now all of them have good English. They can understand that the English person wants the window closed, but do they catch all the other information, th..., the social information? I daresay they probably don't.   5

So, taking this a bit further, Germans for example are seen by the British, erm, especially the English, as abrupt. Why is this? Well, Germans don't usually say 'please'. They issue direct commands. Americans can also seem to British people to be a bit abrupt. Whereas British people, erm, especially the English, well, they can seem horribly obsequious and objectionable to Americans. 'Hey, gosh, why   10
are they being so incredibly polite?' Well the English person just thinks he, or she, is being normally polite. The Japanese or the German again would have a different impression, different interpretation, of what the English person is doing. None of them would necessarily pick up the social origin of the speaker. I mean, they wouldn't know how the different social classes are typically, sort of,   15
indicated in the way people speak.

So what, what are we, what's happening in all this? What's going on? Well, really, what we're doing, we're talking about culture. We're talking about how ways of

speaking English are embedded in the culture of the community. And what do
we mean by culture? Well, we mean a set of expected ways of behaving in given   20
circumstances.

Unit 3, Task 2.1

Interview with Mr Shepherd (11'52")

Interviewer: Mr Shepherd, you're from AERDD. I know that post-graduate
students in your department have to listen to lectures. I wonder if you could
explain how you see those lectures? What is the purpose of a lecture within
your department, or shall we say perhaps a lecture generally?

Mr Shepherd: Erm, well I think different people will have different ideas on this,   5
but I would suggest that erm, er the reason for lectures is that the, the subject
areas that the students are, are studying are, are so large that er, the, the
lecture, or the lecturers erm, provide a summary of erm, er of the key ideas,
the main theories, er, to give a broad framework for the, for the students to, to
er, to read and broaden their study of that particular area.   10

Interviewer: So it's, it would seem that it's perhaps not specifically knowledge-
based, but more it's, it's looking at something broader than just the transmission of factual information.

Mr Shepherd: Erm, yes, I th..., I think er, the lecturer will present factual information, but what essentially they're trying to do is to er, to articulate the   15
different arguments, the different kind of theories that exist within a subject
area, so the student has some, erm, understanding of the basic ideas so that
they can then explore the literature.

Interviewer: Are there different kinds of lectures, or different kinds of listening
situations?   20

Mr Shepherd: Erm, in, at AERDD I suppose there are broadly two. There are
lecturers, or lectures, which may be given by erm, the staff of the department
or by outside speakers, and there are seminars and group work, erm, where
the, the students will be er, listening and working with their fellow students.

Interviewer: So if we could just concentrate on lectures for a moment. Are all   25
those lectures similar?

Mr Shepherd: Er, some er, may be defined as rather formal, in the sense that er,
the students have to listen to a, a presentation from a highly structured script,
which has been er, prepared in detail before the lecturer goes in, and then the
lecturer will speak to that script. And that may include periods for questions   30
from the students, and it may be supported by erm, overhead erm, projec-
tions, er slides or erm, er other kinds of er visual material. Erm, whereas other
lecturers, er, have a different style, it's rather, er, less formal, erm, er, perhaps
more interactive and participatory, where what, what they will do, is that they
have a framework of ideas that they will be attempting to, to work through   35
with the students, but this is er, more, er, perhaps a, a series of headings,

which, which they may present on a ho... overhead or they may write up on
the, on a whiteboard, and then they will, then they will discuss these erm, but
perhaps through, partly through a series of, erm, questions to the students so
they present an idea and then question the students about how that fits with
their experience.   40

Interviewer: So within this kind of interactive lecture, there's a, there's a role for
the students to make their own contribution and in some way to shape the
lecture? Or is that perhaps taking that point a little bit too far?

Mr Shepherd: Erm, th... that can happen, erm, if, er, this q... the questions that
the students ask will, erm, allow the lecturer to use that to illustrate, er, the   45
material that, er, he, the lecturer is trying to address. And, indeed if, if, er, this,
it may move, it may mean that perhaps a lecturer hasn't q... perhaps covered
quite the extent of material that they were intending to, in that period. Er, but
they will have a framework that they're trying to work to. If they don't
complete it in that period er, because of this interactive process, then they will,   50
then they will try and make that up in, at a, at a later stage. But it is, er, the
lecturer still is intending to erm, cover a certain amount of material, and erm,
if he doesn't manage it because of that interactive process then it'll be added
into the next session. But it's more flexible.

Interviewer: Would you like to talk a little bit about the advantages or disadvan-   55
tages of one or other of those styles, the, the style which uses a more prepared
script, compared to the more interactive style where there is more place for the
students to make their contribution?

Mr Shepherd: Erm, yes, I suppose, I haven't really thought about this before, but
erm, I suppose that erm, the advantage of the interactive style is that er, there's   60
more opportunities, er, for the, for the student to link their experiences with
the, the concepts and the theories that the, the lecturer is, is trying to erm,
present, and gives them a sense of, erm, that the learning is, is a two-way
process, that it isn't simply, erm, the lecturer has all the ideas, all the evidence,
all the material, but that students themselves erm, have, er, experiences which,   65
erm, can help to illustrate those ideas and concepts, but perhaps hadn't
thought about them in that way until, until they attended that, that lecture.
The, the more formal one, erm, perhaps has the advantage of erm, being able
to, if you like, to keep to the framework, to the pattern that the lecturer is
trying to achieve. Erm, and I think that's probably also satisfactory, providing   70
the lecturer has left some time for erm, questions. But I think it, it makes a
much greater distinction between the role of the lecturer and, and the role of
the, of, of the student. One is a, a giver and the other is a receiver. And I
think, at, at a, at post-graduate level, certainly at master's level, erm, we're,
we're not talking about inexperienced, immature people. These are people that   75
have, the students who have a lot of, er, a lot of knowledge and experience
that can, erm, enhance our understanding of the subject area.

Interviewer: Are students able to respond to that, or do some students find that
quite difficult? Because that must be a new experience for many students.

Mr Shepherd: Mm, mm. Some students do respond well to it. I think er, er,   80 others don't. I think it's largely, erm, a, a question of their previous experience. If their, if their previous educational experience has been, er, rather, i... in, a rather formal setting, or what I would see as a rather formal setting, where there has been a clear division between the role of the lecturer and the role of the student, where their role has been to listen, erm, then going into AERDD 85 where there is a, an implication, there is almost a requirement, a, an understanding that they have to contribute to the process, that can be quite threatening if they, if they don't have that experience. Also, many, because of the formal er, erm, their experience of formal, er lecturing in the past, they erm, the, they don't know what is expected of them, they don't th..., they 90 think of the subject area as being very clearly defined, whereas in, at post-graduate level, what we're trying to say is that, that, er, this is, er, our development of understanding of subject areas is, is, grows, it, it isn't, it isn't complete, there isn't a beginning or a middle or an end, and, that, at, at post-graduate level, what we're trying to do is to, to get them to recognise that erm, that this 95 is exciting, that they can devise their own understanding of the subject area, and that's partly what the process is about.

Interviewer: You mentioned also seminars. They presumably contribute, in a somewhat different way, to this understanding that students have of their subject.

Mr Shepherd: Yes, I think, I think one of the advantages we like to think that we 100 have at AERDD is that, because we have, er, a wide range of students from different countries and different backgrounds, is that this provides an opportunity f... for students to learn from one another. Erm, a student may present a seminar on a, on a, a, an issue that they're facing, in the, in their work, and attempt to relate that to, to theories and ideas, erm, in the subject 105 area. And other students may actually be experiencing similar problems, erm, but have addressed them in different ways, because of the, the, the context and the circumstances that they're working in. And it's very useful for the students to, er, to learn from one a... one another about how they've experienced these different issues, and how they've dealt with them. 110

Interviewer: Seminars are always student-led?

Mr Shepherd: Erm, there are different kinds of seminars, b... th.... we have one set of seminars which are essentially student-led. There is a member of staff in there, who, erm, perhaps will initiate the first set of seminars but after that, er, then, they are managed by the students. Erm, and so, each one of the students 115 will have an opportunity to make a presentation during a term. Er, but there are other seminars which are, say, presented by erm, er, research students, erm, do...er, who are doing er, P... M.Phils and PhDs, and erm, they are then presenting, er, the progress that they're making in their, in their research.

Interviewer: How do students respond to seminars? Do they find them difficult 120 in any respect?

Mr Shepherd: Erm, broadly speaking, my experience is that th... the students enjoy them, and most of them cope with them quite well. But some of them are, erm, slightly er, worried about it. I mean if they haven't had any experience of, of standing up in public and making a presentation, but at 125

AERDD, the seminar groups are quite small, there may be only six to ten students, and by the time that they er, they er, are involved in the seminar programme, the students have begun to get to know one another, and they're, they're very non-threatening. Er, erm, there's no er, problem about making mistakes. I...i...it's, it's all about learning from one another. 130

Interviewer: Could I just ask you briefly about the use of, erm, visual aids and transparencies and handouts. What's your own use of those and what's your view on the usefulness of them for students?

Mr Shepherd: Erm, well I use, I d... I do use, erm, handouts, and erm, and over-heads. Erm, I will, very often I will make transparencies that have got erm, a, a 135 key idea, er, on that, expressed in perhaps two or three lines, which I will then project, and then I will talk around that idea. Erm, the overhead gives a focus to, a, a reminder to the student of, of the idea that we're, that I, that I'm trying to convey, and it gives them an opportunity to write it down, to copy that. Erm, the overheads that I use tend also to be s..., er, summaries of the 140 key points that I want to make, in a lecture. But I also, I als... er, I also use erm, handouts which erm, may be, may be fuller than that, erm, but give more detail of a particular point, maybe erm, an, a small extract from, from a book or a piece of the literature.

Interviewer: Would you give these handouts before the lecture, so that students 145 could prepare before they came in?

Mr Shepherd: Some. I will give some handouts, perhaps a handout on a case study that we intend to discuss in a following lecture, and er, I will give that out the week before so that they could, they've read it, or should have read it, and they've then got some idea, of the, of the material that we're going to 150 discuss. Th...the handouts which erm, are, are, are more like summaries of, of the key points in a lecture, I will give at the end of the lecture, because I find otherwise the students get them and then they tend to be reading them rather than listening, and I think the important, erm, process they should be going through is listening to what's being said, by the lecturer and i... in the discus- 155 sion with the, with the students in the class.

UNIT 3, TASK 3.2
See lines 42–78 above, (25'8")

Cassette 1, side 2
UNIT 3, TASK 4.1

Intercultural communication (2'41")

Lecturer: Now, erm, if we take erm, Japanese culture for example, erm I think there's even a, a Japanese word for, for this, *amae*, I think it is, erm where you've got the idea of dependence of a subordinate on a superior. Erm, it's, it's basically, it's modelled on the, er, parental relationship. So you've got the

parent exercising a benign authority over the dependent child, and the child 5
accepting this dependency. Erm, so i... it is actually a, a sort of two-way street.
It's, it's not just that you've got a superior who, er, kind of orders people
around. Erm, it's also, concerned with the sense that this is accepted, and that
these people, the subordinate party is prepared to, erm, accept that authority
and is dependent upon it. Now erm, Joan, you said you thought that, that 10
erm, Ireland was...

Student 1: Yes, I think that Ireland is probably low power distance, because
people are not very dependent on authority.

Lecturer: Uh-huh. Erm, so they're...

Student 1: I think they're quite erm, individualistic and even though they might 15
pay lip service to authority and appear to accept what's been said, I think then
they will turn around and do their own thing.

Lecturer: Well, that's an example I guess of where people in a way say one thing
and do another, where there may be, at one level an acceptance of er, power
distance, but in people's actual behaviour, erm, really almost a, erm, subversion 20
of, the, of power distance.

Student 2: It's the subversive Irish again.

Lecturer: [*Laughter*] Ha, well. Maybe er, we have to be careful that we don't slip
into stereotypes, and this of course is the danger of, or the limitation of erm,
setting up these cultural dimensions, is that they can be seen or even be used 25
to, er, support stereotypes, so one has to be very careful, erm at looking at
these, particularly as Hofstede shows, there is a, a kind of different erm,
constellations, or configurations of these different dimensions. Erm, and
talking of er, these dimensions, perhaps we'd better move on now to looking at
erm, individualism and collectivism. 30

UNIT 3, TASK 5.2

Returning to study (2'28")

Right, I'd like to talk to you today, about an experience that I had when I first
started my MA, and I came back after having been away from the university for
quite a long time, working, I'd been away for nearly ten years, between the time
when I did my BA and the time that I did my MA, and erm, I'd like to know if
any of you have had the same experience, if you're going through the same thing 5
at the moment. Now, I found it really hard to sit down in a lecture, and listen
and understand and take notes at the same time, and when I'd done my BA, ten
years before, it's something that I'd done with absolutely no problem, so, you
know, I was really surprised, and I just couldn't understand what the difficulty
was. Erm, I noticed that my notes, for example, were absolutely voluminous. I 10
filled pages and pages, virtually copying down everything I heard. I think this is
what I was doing, I was copying down everything the lecturer was saying, and
copying down too much, I could tell myself in fact. Erm, but I just wasn't

confident enough really to cut down on what I was doing. Er, I wasn't sure what I needed, and what I didn't need, and I just couldn't stop taking these e... enor- 15
mous, voluminous notes.

So gradually, what happened, I think there was a breakthrough at a certain point. Erm, what happened was this. I noticed that all the lectures more or less followed the same kind of pattern in my department. Erm, I mean I'd say there's almost an unofficial structure to the proceedings. Now once I realised this I knew that 20
each lecture was going to be the same. It was going to start off with a bit of revi-sion, and then there was going to be an introduction, stating why something's important or interesting or relevant, and then, there was going to be a theory, and the theory has examples and counter-examples, and this then gives rise to a new theory with examples and counter-examples, and so on, and I realised that 25
most of the lecturers mo..., more or less followed this kind of pattern. So, I think gradually I just realised what I needed to do was write down the main points, and then for me the notes were much easier to read and to use, they were much more efficient, and in fact, the listening, the whole listening process, listening to the lectures, erm, was just a lot easier, I felt much more confident about it and it 30
just became much more accessible for me.

INTERLUDE 1: 1. Putting the military into print (5'41")

TASK 2.1: The first extract

Military regimes in Latin America have often been described from an historical perspective, and most people are probably familiar with the names and possibly some of the main events associated with these regimes.

There is another interesting way of finding out about these regimes though – another way of seeing just what the military presence in Latin America has really 5
meant. This is through the literary productions of the time, taking a literary perspective on the people and the events. This is exactly what I want to talk about today.

Let me start by giving some brief background to these military regimes. Generally speaking, they span the period from the sixties to the early eighties, 10
because it is precisely in the early eighties when most countries returned to democracy. Now if you ask me why, why the military came into power, well, there would be very..., various reasons, and of course different commentators will explain these slightly differently. Mainly though, it was because these countries were experiencing political, social and economic unrest at that time. Of course 15
no doubt many sociologists would like to suggest that these countries are more military than civilian in their ideology. Well, they might be right, particularly when you compare Latin America with, let's say, North America, the United States. But I'm not going to get into that particular argument at the moment.

The countries I am referring to today are Chile, Argentina and Uruguay, although we could take examples from other Latin American countries as well, such as Colombia and Peru. Now, let me concentrate on the social impact of the military regimes in these countries. A military coup brought with it oppression, not only social but also intellectual oppression. It also meant poverty and exile. These consequences, if I might put it that way, these results of the military presence, are reflected in the works of Borges in Argentina, Isabelle Allende in Chile, and Mario Benedetti in Uruguay. 20

25

TASK 3.2

The rest of the talk

So, let's start by talking about Borges, who could perhaps be called the 'aristocratic humanitarian'. Now, why do I choose that particular label for Borges? It's not, of course, to suggest that it is unusual for aristocratic people to be humanitarian. It's just that the aristocracy of Latin America didn't really suffer the consequences of the military regimes. To a large extent, I think they were protected, and this is what makes Borges so interesting. Although he belonged to the Argentinean aristocracy, he was very sensitive to the suffering that others, ordinary people, were really undergoing. In his poetry Borges shows the social life of the time, and we can see this recognition of the suffering of the ordinary people. His poetry acts as a sort of mirror to poverty and social oppression, which are the two consequences of these military regimes that we identified just a minute ago. 5

10

If we go to Chile, then of course we find Isabel Allende. We would all recognise her, I think, as a human rights supporter. She writes about injustices to people with high ideals, and about people who believed in human rights, and that, I think, is very important. In her novels, she always writes about freedom of speech, and love for life over death. You may have seen the movie of one of her books. It's *The House of the Spirits*, and this is a good example of her work, and the concern for human rights that you find there, specially in Chile. 15

Now, in Uruguay, we find the third of the writers that we are talking about today, and that's Benedetti, Mario Benedetti. I tend, er, to call, er, Benedetti 'the voice of the oppressed', because, er, this is the way I just see him. In his short stories, he shows the suffering of those who oppose the military regimes. We can also see there, the exile, and the loneliness, and the longing of all these people to return to their homeland. 20

Well, that's just a very quick look at three Latin American writers, and at the way they responded in their writing to the military regimes in their respective countries. What you need to do now is to read their works for yourselves if you can, and look at these themes, and the way in which these regimes in Latin America affected the lives of the people who live under them. 25

INTERLUDE 1: 2. Definitely not England (8'33")

TASK 2.2: The first extract

I'm going to talk today, for a few moments, about a small country called Wales. Wales is on the western side of Great Britain, right next to England, with which it has a common border of, erm, something like 300 kilometres, I think. Erm, the history of modern Wales is very much tied up with that of England. Er, the Act of Union, which was about the middle of the sixteenth century, brought the two countries together, and for much of that time the history of Wales has tended to be one of the decline of national identity, until we get to the nineteenth century, when there was a sudden resurgence in nationalism, which took place, I think, across the whole of Europe at that time.

5

TASK 3.2

The second extract

The geography of Wales, first then. The geography of Wales is that it's a rather hilly and mountainous country, the highest point being Snowdon, which is, er, something like, er, 3000 feet, er, which is approximately 4500 kilometres, er, above sea level. Er, in the south of Wales there are moorlands and valleys, and it's, erm, reasonably rich farming country, a..., at least in the south-west. The south-east of Wales is where, particularly in the nineteenth century, there was a great deal of heavy industry, that's to say coal-mining and steel production. Indeed the town of Merthyr Tydfil at one point in the nineteenth century was, I think, er, the major steel producer in the world, producing more steel than any other town. However, in the second part of the twentieth century, heavy industry in South Wales went into considerable decline, as indeed it did in most of Europe at that time. Er, deep coal mines have almost disappeared. I, I think there's still one deep mine left, er, at the moment, but they have virtually disappeared. And the steel-making industry has also contracted considerably. Er, there is, in fact, extremely high male unemployment in the ex-industrial areas of South Wales these days. To some extent the unemployment has been dented by new industries, er, concerned with computers and silicon chips and such likes, er, and in particular, the Japanese have invested very heavily in South Wales. Er, however, most of the jobs in computers and silicon chips and that sort of thing, er, tend to be, er, jobs for women, rather than for unemployed miners. Erm, nonetheless, er, it has helped significantly to, to give employment, and I think there are more Japanese companies in South Wales than anywhere else in the United Kingdom at the moment.

5

10

15

20

Erm, one of the, the most, er, distinctive features of Wales i... is of course the language. Out of the present population of approximately two and a half million, around one-fifth, that's to say around twenty percent, er, speak Welsh as a first language, and quite a few of the rest have learned Welsh a... as a second

25

language. Er, the language is of course completely different from English. If I can
say a few words, for example 'be di'r amser?' means 'What time is it?' in Welsh,
and 'How are you?' is, er, 'sut 'dach chi?', er, at least in the northern dialect, and
'shw ma'i?' in the southern dialect. Primary education, er, through the medium   30
of Welsh, er, has always been possible, in practice, and the use of Welsh as a
medium of instruction has increased rapidly since 1947, when the first official
Welsh medium school, or 'ysgol gymraeg', as they are known, er, was set up, er,
in the town of Aberystwyth. There are now several hundred Welsh-medium
primary schools throughout Wales, and also a few Welsh-medium secondary   35
schools as well. Indeed, in the University of Wales it's possible to pursue a degree
in the Humanities entirely through the medium of Welsh. Erm, but not, er, as
far as I gather, in the Sciences, where English is absolutely necessary.

From, er, [cough] the point of view of politics, the Welsh language has been
something of a double-edged sword. It helps to give th... the country identity on   40
the one hand, but on the other hand it does divide Wales, into the Welsh-
speaking Welsh and the non-Welsh-speaking Welsh. Now, the non-Welsh-
speaking Welsh, the English mono-linguals, have always been very suspicious of
any move in Wales towards political autonomy or independence, because th...,
they are afraid that as non-Welsh-speakers, they might end up second-class citi-   45
zens in their own country. I..., indeed, there is, I suppose, a, an element of justification in this view. Er, it is certainly of advantage in many parts of Wales to be
able to speak Welsh, er, for local government, and, erm, al..., also e..., educational
purposes. Many education authorities in Wales, for example, will not employ
teachers unless they speak Welsh, or have passed the Welsh GCSE examination.   50

TASK 3.3

The final extract

Erm, as far as present trends in the economy go in Wales, I've already mentioned
that heavy industry has gone into decline. Agriculture, however, er, still does
reasonably well, although some hill farmers in north Wales have suffered considerably, apparently because of the fallout from the Chernobyl accident in what
was the USSR, several years ago. Ever since the Chernobyl disaster, around thirty   5
farmers in north Wales have been un..., unable to sell their sheep, er, on the open
market, but have simply had to sell them to the government who then kill them
and burn them. Er this apparently is because the sheep's, er, meat is too heavily
contaminated, erm, and the meat is contaminated because the moorlands where
the sheep graze has been made radioactive by the rain that fell after the   10
Chernobyl nuclear plant accident. Erm, that said, however, a number of Welsh
nationalists have pointed out that these Welsh hill farms are all very close to the
nuclear processing plant in Trawsfynydd, so it may well be that Chernobyl is
simply a convenient excuse perhaps, for something, the real cause of which is
closer to home.   15

Er, as far as south Wales goes, as I said heavy industry has gone into a decline, and to a certain extent agriculture there has also suffered. Er, dairy farmers have had a hard time because milk prices have fallen in recent years, and of course beef farmers have gone through a particularly bad patch, er, because of mad cow disease and the restrictions o..., on the sale of beef and beef-related products. 20

The brighter picture, which I was speaking about, of Japanese investment in south Wales, has of course also, in very recent years, come to something of a halt, because of the economic problems, er, in the Far East, erm, so that, er, the general picture i..., is not perhaps as bright now as it may have been a couple of years back. Tourism, of course, is, er, always there in Wales. Er, in the past, er, 25 many areas of north Wales, and to some extent the west coast have relied very heavily on tourism. Er, tourism, of course, is something of a double-edged sword again, because very often tourists destroy the very thing which they have come to see. And what they come to see in Wales very often is, er, isolated and empty countryside. Of course, if too many tourists come, the country is no longer 30 isolated and empty.

So, all in all, what we have in Wales at the moment is a pretty mixed picture, erm, and of course, this is the case for so many of the world's countries.

UNIT 4, TASK 1.2

Global climate change (0'20")

Many of you come from cities which are rather polluted. We've been hearing on the radio over the past few days about quite bad air pollution in London, for example. I'm not concerned immediately with that kind of city-scale pollution, so the pollution which is confined to a city, I'm thinking more, more on the global scale about the way human activity may be changing the global 5 atmosphere.

UNIT 4, TASK 2.2

1. Britain and European Monetary Union (2'21")

O.K., good morning. Well, first up, can you all hear me? Good. Well that's a good place to start. Well today I'm going to be talking to you mainly about Britain and EMU, Ec..., European Monetary Union. Basically, how the UK is thinking about the issue of the European single currency and what Britain's preparations for involvement in that process are going to be. 5

First though, before I give you the structure of the lecture, I'm going to give you some kind of introductory context. The first thing that you really need to know or remember, is that the UK attitude towards European integration has always

been very ambiguous. It..., the UK didn't join when the Coal and Steel
Community was set up in 1951, or when the Economic Community was set up   10
in '57. We tried to join twice later on, but were turned down, twice, by the
French under General de Gaulle, because he thought that the UK was far too
centred on the US, and wasn't ready to be a European partner.

The second thing you need to know is that the single currency has been a dream
of European integrationists for a very long time. Apart from general ideas about   15
how nice and useful it might be, there have been hard plans put forward for this
since the summit in the Hague, in the Netherlands, in 1969. There have been
several attempts to make the idea a reality but they haven't worked until now.
Initially, of the fifteen member states of the European Union, eleven will be
taking part in the single currency. What this means is the EU will have a single   20
currency bloc with four member states outside, and for the time being the UK is
one of those states outside.

So, what am I going to do within this context? We're going to look at three
things today. Firstly, what we're going to do is look at some EU history since the
single European Act in the mid-1980s, so you can understand how this prospect   25
of a single currency has finally become a reality. Next up, we're going to look at
the UK and its general attitude and involvement with the EU, and then finally
we're going to narrow the focus down and look particularly at the UK and EMU.

2. Globalisation (1'14")

Globalisation. This is often said to be the most profound and wide-ranging
change of our time. It's said to be something which affects everybody's life; that
affects people as diverse as farmers in the third world, stockbrokers in London
and New York; or global tycoons with multi-million dollar media empires. So,
obviously, this is something about which a political scientist, or, for that matter, a   5
historian, or sociologist, or geographer, or a whole range of other disciplines,
might well be interested.

And I'm going to try to give you, today, some understanding of what globalisation is, and what its implications could be for the world.

So I'm going to talk on a global scale, and I'm going to traverse some fairly long   10
periods of time and some fairly wide spaces in doing that.

3. Soil Science (1'08")

Well, what I want to do this afternoon is deal, just briefly, with soil erosion in
general, and then illustrate some of the points I've made, with reference to the
United Kingdom. Now, you may not think that, in the United Kingdom, soil
erosion is a problem. Well, I'm going to suggest to you, this afternoon, that with
our relatively shallow soils, soil erosion is potentially a major problem for farmers   5
in the United Kingdom.

So this is what I'm going to do this afternoon. I'm going to structure my talk with a brief introduction of soil erosion, and then look specifically at soil erosion in the United Kingdom. This arises out of some research I've been doing, in the past, rather a long time ago now, but, nevertheless, some work I was involved with, with other colleagues in the United Kingdom.   10

What I'm going to do, is, illustrate where the farmer produces the soil erosion, where he, through his actions, mismanages the land, and produces soil erosion which may be small each time, but in the long run may have a substantial impact on his agricultural potential, and the overall farm productivity.   15

UNIT 4, TASK 2.3

Eyewitness Testimony (1'55")

This lecture is on eye-witness testimony.

In a court of law, one of the most effective ways of establishing a person's guilt, is by finding an individual who actually witnessed the crime, and who can then identify the defendant as the criminal. A great deal then, depends on the accuracy of the eye-witness's testimony. Let's consider the case of Keith Carroll.   5
He was accused of armed robbery. One witness identified him as the criminal. He was convicted and spent two years in prison, claiming that he was innocent. In fact, it turned out that he was innocent, and another person confessed to the crime that he was supposed to have committed.

Let's consider another case of a man who took the law into his own hands, and   10
acted as witness, judge and executioner. One night Claude Breton was attacked, and beaten up, by a taxi-driver. About a year later, he was sitting in a bar, when he saw the man that had beaten him up. He went home, got a gun, came back, shot and killed the man. The problem was, that this was another case of mistaken identity. It turned out that this could not have been the man, and   15
indeed this person was not even a taxi-driver.

Mistaken identification is one of the major reasons for wrongful conviction.

Cassette 2, side 1
UNIT 4, TASK 3.1

Economics Lecture (4'51")

O.K. Well, as you'll have seen already I have a number of, I had a number of announcements to give at the beginning of today's lecture, and, therefore, my intention is, in relation to the first of, of six topics this term, to give that topic over a course of two weeks, two lectures, this week and next, before proceeding to the

remaining, er, five topics for this term in the other five weeks. Erm, and, you'll see 5
from the handout, that today's topic is a general one, which will relate, to some
extent, to the work you have already covered in the first year part of your course.
And this is intentional, erm, you will have gathered already from first year
Economics, that macro-economics tends to proceed by way of the analysis of the
specific components of aggregate demand, and so for much of this term, we will 10
cover, one week at a time, the major, or principal, components of aggregate
demand in the economy. However, my intention today is to talk a little bit, by way
of introduction, as to how macro-economics came to be structured in this way,
how the various components of aggregate demand came to play such a prominent
role in discussions of the macro-economy. This owes largely to the contribution of 15
John Maynard Keynes in the 1930s, who suggested, not only demand management
policies on the part of governments, but also, that, erm, the analysis of the
economy should proceed by way of an analysis of the various elements of aggregate
demand – consumption demand, investment demand and the demand for money.
Erm, and, I will talk today, and next week, in relation to topic one, about the 20
contribution of Keynes and of some of the predecessors of Keynes, going back for
instance, as far as Adam Smith, and other writers, erm, many years previously,
before explaining how the work of Keynes has led into the present day.

From here, erm, in the third week, concerning topic two, we shall then turn to
an analysis of aggregate supply, for which we will need just one week at this 25
stage, and then, deal with the various components of aggregate demand, one
lecture at a time, erm, investment demand, money demand and the consumption
function. And then, at the end of the, er, term, in the final lecture, we shall
address the issues of the overall system of aggregate demand, bringing these
various components together, erm, in the form of the IS-LM analysis, and then 30
the relationship between that structure of aggregate demand and the aggregate
supply, erm, schedules, looking at the interaction between aggregate demand and
aggregate supply.

Next term, we will then go one step further, to look at the various dimensions of
aggregate demand and aggregate supply, in an international context, which is 35
important today, in view of the globalisation of the world economy, and the
much greater degree of international interdependence between national
economies than applied in the past.

And then, in the following term, in the Lent term, we shall address, erm, policy
questions that derive from this analysis, principally policy questions related to 40
how we might reduce the level of unemployment, and reduce the level of infla-
tion, in the, erm, economy, erm, which will extend the analytical part of our
discussion, in the second term of the course, and demonstrate how it applies to
current day policy questions.

Well, that's an outline of where the course will go. Erm, today, however, I shall 45
proceed with a more detailed, erm, discussion of the history of macro-economic
thought.

Unit 5, Task 1.4

Higher Education (8'49"): The first extract

A variety of arguments have been put forward for the purposes of a university, a..., and this summarises some of them. [*Reads from OHT1*]. Erm, we're here to gain knowledge for knowledge's own sake. Er, some people would argue that we're here to preserve the culture, that somehow or other we're a museum of history. Others would argue we're not just here to preserve it but to somehow   5
keep it pure, to be a kind of gatekeeper on the truth. Another argument is that we're here in the pursuit of excellence, that is somehow to be a beacon of what is best in everything. And of course, those who pay us in particular, would argue that we're here to serve the community. Now, in some sense, all of those a..., are true. But one thing isn't true. We, we're not here just to preserve it. If that were   10
true we, we wouldn't need the people, I mean the library does that very well, the library preserves knowledge. Look at this, this is a quotation from Bruner. He says [*reads from OHT2*], 'A body of knowledge, enshrined in a university faculty and embodied in a series of authoritative volumes, is the result of much prior intellectual activity. To instruct someone in these disciplines is not a matter of   15
getting him to commit results to mind, but rather it is to teach him to partici- pate in the process that makes possible the establishment of knowledge. We teach a subject, not to produce little living libraries on that subject, but rather to get a student to think mathematically for himself, to consider matters as a historian does, to take part in the process of knowledge-getting. Knowledge is a process   20
not a product.' And that sums up a large reason as to why you are here. It gives the educational reasons for a university. Now, that doesn't mean to say, we mustn't forget, that they can also be useful. A... and what's interesting, all things are useful. Erm, I doubt you'd find it difficult to imagine that an Agricultural Faculty is useful, that Science is useful, and we all know that Technology's useful.   25
Mm, but how about the Arts? How about Art itself? Well, maybe that's useful too, and, and here is a quotation from the Scottish Council for Research in Education, looking at curricula things, in 1931, which addresses why Art might be useful. [*Reads from OHT3*] 'While it will of course be readily admitted that not all are equally gifted aesthetically, even pupils with no special skill in Art may   30
gain much from associating with those who are producing fine work. By such contact something of the interest which makes for understanding and apprecia- tion is readily communicated. Such pupils may in after life attain positions of influence in industry, in educational affairs, or in public life, in which if they lack aesthetic development, they may prove a danger to the community. And they do   35
constitute a danger, and by their indifference to natural or architectural beauty, may be the means of permanently disfiguring a countryside or a city.' A powerful argument that everyone should study Art, because if you don't, you may be a danger. Well, we would expect, therefore, the id..., the purpose of a university to include knowledge for knowledge sake, the education of individuals, and this   40
usefulness idea and of course serving the community.

UNIT 5, TASK 2.2

The second extract

And this is a big task, a, a very big task. You can see that there's a mixture of the
cultural and the useful, and a university int... education is undoubtedly useful.
Having a degree is good for getting a job. So clearly it has a utilitarian value for
the individual. And for some of you these might be telling statistics. Erm, look at
this one [*refers to OHT4*]. This one refers to the percentage of the population in   5
higher education, that are in less developed, in developing, and in industrialised
countries, and you can see it steadily goes up, it steadily rises. And as a conse-
quence of that rise, look at this graph [*refers to OHT5*] of the number of scientists per one thousand of the population, and again you can see, a dramatic rise,
from only a few, less than ten, in less developed countries, through to over a   10
hundred in industrialised countries. And compare those with this graph of life
expectancy in years [*refers to OHT6*] and the correlation is pretty startling. In less
developed countries, we've got something in just the mid-fifties, and it rises until
the late seventies. There's something like twenty-two odd years more, to be happy
in. Well, at least we hope we'll be happy. So, clearly, level of education matters.   15
And I thought you'd enjoy the answer our Vice Chancellor gave to a question,
when he was asked what was the degree for? Now he said, for his own part, he
believed that ideally it should derive from an academically rigorous course,
including basic factual knowledge, problem solving, general fluency and
numeracy, and he told us that students should be helped to develop personal and   20
presentational skills and stamina. And those of you going on to study here, well,
there's a warning of how difficult it's going to be.

UNIT 5, TASK 3.2

The final extract

It's extremely important to realise th... that a university is the people in it. It's not
the buildings, it's not the grounds. A university is a society, a corporate body, a, a
community of people. And what do those people have in common? Well, obviously they're all studying, but that's true of other educational institutions,
schools, further education, etc. So what characterises a university, as opposed to   5
other educational institutions? Well, I, I think we'd say as a general answer, that
in a university everyone is to some extent engaged in research. It's concerned with
research. Everyone has an interest in discovering new things or shedding new
light on what's already known. Everybody. O.K? All of us. Now..., and we do
that in a variety of ways. Undergraduates, for example, as they arrive from   10
school, in their first year in particular, they'll not be directly carr..., concerned
with carrying out any research themselves. No, that part of the work, under-grad-
uates, is more characterised by trying to deal with complexities, with a... a...
additional variations to school work, to take into account more dimensions,

more aspects, more variables. But it is intended that by the time they reach their   15
third year, their last year, they will have reached a point of realising that not
everything is known, that they've begun to grapple with the fact that there isn't
always an answer, so that the course is designed so undergraduates will reach the
point where they know, where they come to realise, that research is necessary.
When we go on to postgraduates, master's students, we'd expect them not only to   20
know what is known, but also to know what is not known, now of course I don't
mean, by that, that they know the answer to something that is not known, but
they know that nobody knows the answer. And so we would characterise a
master's student as not just knowing what is known, which an undergraduate
might, but also being more strongly aware of what is known, the extent of what   25
is known, and knowing where to find it. If you're going on to a Ph.D. then you
are going to be expected to make an original contribution to knowledge. So of
course you're involved in research, because new knowledge is what you're going
to have to do. And that's true of the staff as well. We also have an obligation to
know new things. But more than that, to also know when they're worthwhile and   30
to encourage worthwhile new knowledge, to be able to evaluate it and to publish
it. So the staff should be able to do those other things, but also to evaluate the
status of that knowledge, and whether it's worthwhile. This is sometimes play-
fully described as undergraduates learn what others have said, and everybody
agrees with, master's students learn what others have said, even if some people   35
disagree with it, Ph.D. students say it, and the staff tell you whether it's worth
saying or not. O.K., that's playful, but it does come from a serious analysis of
what we're trying to do.

Unit 6, Task 1.1

Vocabulary for listening (6'33")

Today I'd like to talk about the importance of vocabulary development for academic listening.

There's been a, a lot of research recently into the importance of vocabulary for
reading, and it's now pretty widely recognised that below a certain vocabulary
threshold, it's just not possible to read effectively, well that is, if you don't know   5
enough vocabulary, enough words, you, you can't read well.

Now if you think about it, there are great similarities between reading and
listening, they're both receptive skills, that is the student's not actually required to
produce language, like you do with, erm, speaking and writing. With reading,
you just have to understand the written word, and with listening, obviously you   10
have to understand the spoken word. Well I'd like to argue that er, although
vocabulary is important for reading it's even more important for listening and I
think there are several really important reasons for this.

First of all, when er, when you're reading it's possible to control the speed at which you read, so if you're having difficulty, you don't understand something, you can read it more slowly or you can read it again. This of course isn't possible when you're listening, because if you think, during a lecture, you have to understand what the lecturer is saying at the speed the lecturer speaks. Now that can be a speed of up to 300 syllables per minute. So, you see it's very important to be able to understand the vocabulary automatically, you, you don't have time to think about it.

Secondly, the, the things that help er, people speak with natural rhythm in English, the features of connected speech, make it even more difficult. Now, erm, I'm sure you're all sure, all familiar with contractions, so instead of saying *it is*, you say *it's*, well that's one of the features of connected speech, but there are other things like, er, weak forms, so we don't say *and*, we say *'nd*, we don't say *of*, we say *'v*. Er, there are several other types of erm, features of connected speech, things like linking. This is particularly im..., difficult for some students. If you think of *first of all*, so it's three words, but when it's spoken it sounds like one, *firstofall* – there's no, no pause between the words. This is particularly difficult for students who are used to reading and writing, they're more familiar with the written word.

I'd like to draw a sort of parallel to help you imagine it. If you think, if in written language, some of the phrases were written without any spaces between the words, that's more or less what it's like for listening.

Er, the next aspect which makes it more difficult is, is the speakers themselves. If you think about it, lecturers may have different accents, they may speak more or less clearly, and again, to make this easier to understand, I'll, I'll tell you what it would be like in writing. If you think, for different accents, it would be like different styles of handwriting, erm, some of which are more legible, easier to read, than the others, and with er, respect to clarity of speech, obviously some people speak more clearly than others and, a parallel in writing would be if some of the words on the page were badly printed or, they'd been almost completely rubbed off.

And then finally there's noise. Now obviously you can have noise when you're reading, but if you do, and you get distracted, you can go back and read that bit again. But when you're listening to a lecture, there may be noise from other students coming in late, or whatever, and the lecturer will continue speaking, you can't ask the lecturer to stop and repeat it, you simply miss that part of the talk, and of course that part may be one of the most important parts. And if you think about a, a parallel in reading, that would be like trying to read with smoke drifting across the page, but without being able to go back and look at it again.

So, as you can see it's essential to be able to understand vocabulary automatically, you don't have time to think about it. So, the question is, what can students do to extend their vocabulary? Well first of all there are two different types of vocabulary, if you think general English, that everybody uses, and er, academic English, so what you need for your studies. For general English there are a number of er, really good dictionaries, the most modern dictionaries include things like topic pages, all the words connected with travel, or whatever. Er, there are quite a lot of good vocabulary books, and there are even students' thesauri – these are dictionaries which are arranged by meanings, so for example, different ways of expressing need in English. Erm, they also have things arranged by topic, so, for example, the environment. 60

With regard to academic vocabulary, there are lists of the most common words used in academic English, and of course these are very beneficial.

So, as it's so important to understand new vocabulary when it's spoken, you need to know how to pronounce the new vocabulary, the new words, so I'd strongly 65 recommend learning the phonemic symbols. Er, you can find them at the beginning of a dictionary with example words. In that way, once you know them, you, you know how to pronounce any new words. And there are also some CD ROM dictionaries now, which actually have the words recorded by a native speaker, so that's particularly useful. 70

So, as we've seen today, it's, er, vocabulary development is essential for academic listening. Er, it's necessary to be able to understand the lecturer at natural speed, with of course the difficulties we've mentioned of features of connected speech, erm, different accents, different degrees of clarity of speech, and of course the possible distraction of noise in the lecture hall. We've also seen there are many 75 types of, er, material available for you to increase your vocabulary, and of course it's fundamental to listen as much as possible because, as they say, practice makes perfect.

UNIT 6, TASK 2.1

Time and priorities management (8'52")

Today, we're going to talk about managing time and priorities, which is really the same thing, as we'll see I hope by the end of the lecture. Managing time and priorities. And we're going to start from the idea that there's a basic equation in managing time and priorities. Now, don't worry, this is not a mathematics lecture. That is the only equation in this lecture. Work equals time available. 5 Work equals time available. If work equals time available, then we have no problem. It means we have enough time to do all the work that we have to do.

But at times, we all feel that this equation doesn't balance. Managers, for example, usually feel they don't have enough time to do the work they have to do. Students very often feel they don't have enough time to do the work they 10 have to do. We all often find we have a problem with this equation. The equation doesn't balance. Work doesn't equal the time available. Actually, a very famous man called, er, Northcote Parkinson, said a very cynical thing about the equation. He said that the equation will never balance, because work always

expands to fill the time available. So however much time you've got, work will
always increase to fill that time.   15

O.K, that's a cynical view. Today, I hope we can see a more practical view of how
we can balance the equation. Of course, it may be that you have a genuine
problem. It may be that in your professional life, you have too much work and
not enough time. It may be literally true that you have too much work and not   20
enough time. In that case of course, all you can do is get rid of some of the work
or, somehow, find more time. Today's lecture is not about that problem. Today's
lecture is about the problem, about the idea, that usually the truth is not that
you have too much work or not enough time. The truth is you have not
managed the work or managed your time effectively. The problem is you haven't   25
controlled things, on both sides of the equation. That's the theory behind today's
session.

O.K., let's see how it may be possible to manage each side of the equation. Now,
I'm going to look at this first side, managing the work.

If we want to manage work effectively, we must understand where work comes   30
from. Where does work come from? Maybe that sounds like a stupid question.
Work comes from hundreds of places, of course, hundreds of different sources.
But if we think about those sources for a few moments, we may be able to see
that there are really only two types of work. The first type is your work, work
that you generate, work that you decide on. So Source 1 work, we can call it, is   35
your work, the work you have decided on. As a student, for example, you may
decide what background reading to do for your course. You may decide, from a
number of choices, which assignment to take on, or what project to do. And you
make all sorts of other choices about your work. This Source 1 work we call self-
generated work, work that you generate yourself. You decide you're going to do   40
it. You decide you're going to do it because it meets your aims and objectives,
where you want to go, what you want to achieve. So Source 1 work meets your
aims and objectives. Perhaps we can see now what Source 2 work is. Source 2
work meets other people's aims and objectives. Source 2 work is work which is
given to you by other people, to meet their aims and objectives.   45

Let's look in more detail, at the problem for a student, to see the difference
between these two types of work. For example, the assignment. Is, is an assignment Source 1 work, self-generated, or Source 2 work, given to you by someone
else? Well, clearly, a lot of the work in the assignment is Source 1 work, it's self-
generated. You decide how to actually deal with the assignment. You decide what   50
you're going to do, how you're going to do it. But someone else decides how long
it's got to be, when you've got to hand it in by, how you must present it, in
handwriting, or typing, whether it must be bound, or in manuscript form. So
within the one idea of an assignment, we have Source 1 work and Source 2 work.

Now let's look at the relationship between those two sources. They're related in a   55
very important way. Source 1 work, the work you want to do yourself, self-gener-

ated, Source 2 work, from other people. You start off by doing your Source 1 work. But maybe you get behind in your Source 1 work. Maybe you begin to have a problem with the Source 1 work, and you miss the deadline for handing in part of the assignment or part of the information that your tutor wants. So, you get a   60 memo from your tutor, asking you how you're getting on. That gives you more Source 2 work. You have to answer the memo, you have to deal with the query from your tutor. Maybe in the memo the tutor suggests a meeting. You have to go to the meeting, more Source 2 work. Maybe the tutor suggests you bring a summary of your assignment so far. More Source 2 work. In the meantime, of   65 course, you cannot get on with your Source 1 work. It is a vicious circle. The more Source 2 work you get, the less Source 1 work you can do. And things can get worse and worse and worse. Eventually, you're not doing any Source 1 work at all, you're doing all work that has been given to you by other people. For a student, there's an added problem. When you set out to do an assignment, you are often   70 working with a group of people. They are all answering the same assignment, in their own different ways. But if you get behind in that Source 1 work, you can't call upon the help and, and advice of your colleagues, because they've moved on. They're not doing that assignment any more, they're doing something else.

So, to sum up. On this side of the equation, there are two kinds of work, Source 1   75 work is self-generated, Source 2 work is given to you by other people. If you don't complete your Source 1 work, you will probably have to do more Source 2 work. You'll get more work given to you by other people, and it will become a vicious circle. Eventually, you will have no time for your Source 1 work, at all.

O.K. Let's have a break. After the break, we will look at managing the other side   80 of the equation, the time available.

Unit 6, Task 3.1

Noise experiments (3'06")

O.K. Now, erm, where were we? Right, as I was saying, noise accompanies a great deal of human activity. The question is, does it in general have a positive effect, or, or a negative effect on efficiency? And this is a question that interests a great many researchers. Well, if you were to walk into a computer lab, and see a great number of students who are working with their personal stereos going, you   5 might well conclude that, erm, noise has a positive effect on efficiency. However, it's been shown, in experiments, that performance is adversely affected by continuous loud noise. Well, what happens is that attention tends to be focused on important parts of the task, but the less important features can be overlooked. Th... the mind seems to filter out those less important things, or at least the ones   10 that seem less important at the time, although of course, as we know from our own work, what seems less important, can, can still contribute to a fuller understanding, erm, or fuller performance of, of a particular activity.

What I, what I want to focus on now, however, is some research carried out by Glass and Singer. That, that's on your reading list, Glass and Singer 1971. And 15 their work threw some light on how the context in which noise is experienced is, itself, significant. They demonstrated, Glass and Singer, they demonstrated that especially what a person believes about noise, can affect performance. So, for example, in their experiment, the people, the subjects were told that if they could turn off a noise at any time, the effect it had on performance was less serious. By 20 the way, this didn't actually mean that they turned the noise off. If they could predict when the noise would occur, or if they were led to believe that they could control it, somehow, this also reduced, diminished, the effect of the noise. So the conclusion they came to, and it's been supported by more recent studies, was that people's perception of the extent to which they could control noise, whether they 25 could control it or not, their perception of that, actually reduced the damaging effects on behaviour. So context is important. If, for example, the people who are responsible for a noise are insensitive about the disturbance they're causing, or if people are doing a task and they perceive that the noise in the background is not necessary, or if they're afraid of it, or they think it might have a damaging effect 30 on their health, in all these cases, the negative effects of the noise will be more significant.

UNIT 6, TASK 4.2

Trends in Society (4'43")

That's all I want to say at this point about those two approaches, er, except to suggest that Schumacher's solutions appear to provide our best options for the sustainable use of the world's resources. They're certainly worthy of your attention.

Erm, so much then for the latter years of the twentieth century. But, er, what about the twenty-first century? What, in particular, can we say about those prob- 5 lems that we've identified, problems such as, erm, increasing urbanisation. Will the rapid growth of technology continue? Erm, what directions will scientific discovery take? Erm, I'd like to round off today's discussion by making a few predictions for the next century. They are, of course, just predictions. There's no way that we can, I mean, it's becoming increasingly difficult to make predictions 10 of any kind, even in the short term.

Now as I've stressed to you before, we should never overlook the fact that a theory is scientific to the extent that it is possible to test it. I believe that the following predictions will be supported by evidence that will emerge in the next, er, in the course of the next half century or so. 15

Now since these are mostly developments of a social kind, it's obviously the passage of time we must wait for to throw up the relevant evidence. This of course, as you're well aware, is the case with any non-experimental science, whether it be economics, or astronomy, or whatever. So, then, what are these predictions?

Well, firstly, in the light of what I've already said, I think we will, by the middle   20
of the 21st century, see a reversal of this movement of people to large urban
areas. Now this, I believe, will go hand in hand with increasing political decen-
tralisation, which, erm, er, which will be reflected in, er, in many instances by
increasing federalism. And it will also be accompanied, a..., and I do believe that
this will prove to be highly significant, by radical economic restructuring, coming   25
in the wake of a collapse in capitalism of a rather different order to what people
on the Left predicted for a large part of the 20th century. I suggest to you, that a
complex combination of, er, social, economic and political factors, will bring
about major changes in the way the present system operates. And I think we can
expect a progressive, erm, dissolution, er, disappearance of larger units of produc-   30
tion, with this twentieth-century goal of ever-increasing expansion that er, that
we've been looking at, er, with this goal fast becoming, er, let's say, an anachro-
nism. Whether major shocks to the system will occur along the way, erm, I
mean, in the form, for example, of a, of a world-wide financial crash, is
anybody's guess.   35

So that, then, is my first prediction. Let's look at the second one, a... and obviously this one is not unconnected to what I've just suggested. There will be a
growing, what I'd term, simplification in lifestyle, so that our rather stereotypical,
er, futuristic images of a high-tech 'Space Age' society will, I believe, ring less and
less true. I'm inclined to dismiss, even, er, the idea that such a society will   40
develop in isolation in a, in a few wealthy corners of the globe. I ought to stress
that I don't mean that we're destined to step back into some kind of pre-indus-
trial society. But neither will we all live with more and more life-facilitating
gadgets.

So, let me move on to my third prediction, and here I'll admit I'm really sticking   45
my neck out and you may choose to totally disagree with me, but I'm inclined to
think that science will, in a certain way, become simpler. I don't mean that we
will cease to be scientific in the rigorous manner that has become the hallmark of
good science, but perhaps we'll know better what we can do, and, and what we
can't do with science, and new discoveries, particularly in the fields of physics   50
and er, and also medicine, will support this knowledge.

INTERLUDE 2: 1. Leaping to conclusions (5'48")

TASK 2.1: The first extract

Now, I was, er, travelling abroad, I was in fact attending a conference in a continental, European, country, and I stayed at a hotel in which there was a health spa
complex, attached to the main hotel. Guests could use the facilities, er, which
included a swimming pool. On the, the last morning of a four-day stay, I decided
to have a swim. At seven o'clock I went down to the reception desk in the hotel   5
and told the receptionist that I wanted to use the swimming pool. 'How long are

you staying at the hotel?' she asks. I thought this was an odd question, but I told her I'd been there several days. 'You need a card,' she says, and proceeds to give me a credit card kind of card, a kind of swipe card thing. 'Do I need a towel?' I ask. 'You can get one at the pool,' she answers. So, I go to the health spa building, and down to the ground floor, and here I use the card to go through a turnstile. And I discover that the same card is used to activate the lockers for the safekeeping of valuables. But, I can't see any towels. So, I return to the pool entrance, and ask an attendant for a towel. 'You must pay,' he says. Oh, I think, I don't have any money. And why didn't the hotel receptionist tell me that I had to pay?

So, I returned to the hotel to get some money, but decided that by now, time was passing and I'd already arranged to meet someone for breakfast, so I handed back the card to the receptionist. 'Why didn't you tell me that I had to pay?' I asked. 'Oh, there are so many things to tell the guests,' she says. 'Yes, but it's your job to tell people things like this,' I say.

TASK 2.2

The second extract

Half an hour later, in the dining room, I'm joined by Julie, another guest at the hotel. She'd just been for a swim. 'How was it?' I ask. 'Oh fine,' she says, 'but I had some problems with the arrangements.' 'Oh?' says I. 'Yes. When I went to the receptionist, I asked if the pool was open,' she says. 'The receptionist said it was, but that I needed to pay for a towel. When I got down to the pool, I discovered that I also needed a card to get in.'

TASK 3.3

The final extract

This experience gave rise to several thoughts. Firstly, was this a cross-cultural incident, in which two British people had different expectations from the receptionist, who was a, a, a citizen of the country concerned? Were our expectations based on British notions of hotel service? Did we expect that the job of receptionists was to give as much information as possible to guests, so as to be of help to them? And, what was the expectation of the receptionist? The hotel we were staying in catered to an international clientele, so she was used to dealing with enquiries, presumably, so why didn't she give each of us the information that we needed? Had she been brought up to answer only one question at a time, er, to give information in instalments, only as requested, so when I asked her if I needed a towel, she answered my question with the information she considered appropriate for that query, namely, that towels were available at the pool. Since I

hadn't asked about payment, she didn't tell me that I needed to pay. Or, because she assumed that payment is a normal part of using a hotel swimming pool, she didn't think it was necessary to tell me. Was the communication failure a cultur-   15
ally-based one, or was it simply one of training? Had the receptionist received any training, and if so what training had she received? Had she been trained to answer hotel guests' enquiries as fully as possible, so, when a guest asks about the use of the swimming pool, had she been trained to tell them that they needed a card, and, also, that they needed to pay for the use of a towel? In other words,   20
had she been trained to explain such details in full, and not to assume that guests would already know about such matters?

Now, I think this example illustrates the problem of using incidents like this for making generalisations. Such incidents definitely tell us something about people's behaviour and attitudes, and so they tell us something about culture as well. But   25
I think that to verify our conclusions, we need to observe other incidents, and to question people about their understandings and their motives. In other words, er, before diving into the swimming pool, we need to avoid leaping to premature conclusions.

Cassette 2, side 2
INTERLUDE 2: 2. The Great Hunger (15'13")
TASK 3.1: The first extract

Over the years, the relationship between Britain and Ireland has often been very difficult. Erm, it's been coloured by a number of events, and one of the most profound of those events, I think, was the Great Famine, the, the Great Hunger, which took place in Ireland in the late 1840s and the early 1850s, and in fact it had such a profound effect that it still is remembered with great strong feelings,   5
by many many people in Ireland and all over the world today.

The, we need to go back and see how things were in Ireland at that time. The population, at that stage, in 1845, was approximately eight and a half million, and, of that population, half of it was totally dependent on the potato as their staple diet. It was, really it was a monoculture. Erm, there was about 1.5 million   10
of landless tenants, people who lived on the land which was owned by their land-lord, erm, didn't own the land themselves, and just, er, worked for their landlord and could use a little bit of land to grow whatever crops they needed themselves. So that's 1.5 million landless tenants. There was about another million who owned a little ground of their own, but they were still very dependent on the   15
potatoes that they grew there.

So, you can see that the potato was a very important part of the diet for a large proportion of the population. In fact, they ate it for three meals a day in many cases. I mean, imagine that. The potato, sort of breakfast, lunch and dinner. There's a very interesting statistic, in fact, that, really, seems almost incredible. An   20 average male labourer who was working in the fields could eat six kilos of potato a day. I mean, that seems an incredible amount.

Erm, and it wasn't just important for the people, it was important for the animals as well, because it was, this was what a lot of the animals were fed on. Their main animals that they kept were pigs which they would keep to fatten, but not for themselves to eat. They wanted to fatten the pigs to then sell them, to pay the rent to their landlord. 25

So, you can see that it was important for the people, it was important for the animals. It was a vital part of their economy. So the population was therefore very vulnerable if there was any disease, or anything went wrong with the potato crop. And in 1845, that's exactly what happened. 30

The potatoes were invaded by a kind of fungus, a blight, which, erm, destroyed the potatoes and made them completely inedible. Now this particular disease, this blight, had already struck in Europe, and many peasants in Europe, many of the poor peasants in Europe, had also suffered greatly as a result of it. Erm, but th... the failures were even more catastrophic in Ireland because it happened not only in 1845, but then again in 1846, and this was then followed by a particularly bad winter between 1846 and 1847. So you've got starvation, you've got malnutrition, you've got disease. There was cholera, typhus, smallpox, dysentery. The people were really in a very serious condition, I mean, really suffering greatly as a result of this. Then, 1847, no blight, potato crop was OK. But just as people were getting back on their feet again, then it happened again in '48 and '49, and trailing off, in, er, in, in the west coast of Ireland in, in the early '50s. So, basically, the cumulative effect of all of this, was really devastating on the people. It's estimated that one million of the population died of starvation and disease, I mean, remember that's one million out of 8.5 million of a total population, in really a period of about five, six years. I mean, er, very serious. 35 40 45

TASK 3.2

The second extract

So, let's look at how people tried to help these starving people. First of all, of course, we wonder about the landlords who owned the land, and, er, well, where the poor were living. Now, some did try to help. They provided food, they provided money, they provided clothing, where they could. But that was only a small proportion who actually did make that effort. Many of them didn't do anything whatsoever because, in many cases, they were absentee landlords who actually lived in England, and so, the suffering of the people, er, one point is that the suffering of the people wasn't actually immediately in front of their eyes. But secondly, they were really only interested in the land because of the rent that it brought in. And if the people couldn't pay the rent, they didn't care, they weren't interested. They, erm, instructed their administrators to evict the people if they 5 10 couldn't pay the rent. And in fact, they weren't just evicting the people, I mean throwing them off their land and out of their houses, oh well, their cottages, they were actually destroying the cottages, tumbling them down, so that nobody else could come back in and live in these cottages. Because in fact, in a way, they were trying to clear their land of these, what they saw as useless tenants. So that was very, very bitter, very hard for the people to, to deal with. 15

Task 3.3

The third extract

The other possible source of help, of course, would have been the British government, or th... th...th... the British population, because you have to remember, at that stage, Ireland was governed by Britain, it was ruled by the British government in London.

Now, ah, you have to realise, you have to look at it from the point of view of 5
how people thought of it then. A lot of the politicians, I think, saw it as 'a necessary re-adjustment of the Irish economy'. They saw Ireland as being over-populated and not sufficiently industrialised and they thought that this was just, a, a rather hard way, but a necessary way, of getting rid of a lot of the population and forcing the people to become more industrialised, to leave the land and to go and 10
work in the factories. So, they perhaps appreciated that people were suffering, but they saw it as necessary for political and economic reasons, so they weren't particularly interested in, in sending much help.

Now, the second reason they weren't particularly interested in sending help, was that there was very much an ethos, a belief, that people should be dependent on 15
their own efforts to improve themselves, to, to deal with their own problems. Erm, so they were very unwilling to send help over to them. But, of course, the people that we're talking about in Ireland, the poor people in Ireland at, at the time, were absolutely destitute. They had nothing, they were selling their own clothes to buy food for themselves and their family. So, they didn't really have 20
any resources whatsoever with which to help themselves. And, and perhaps that was not fully appreciated by the British government and the British people at the time.

Thirdly, we have to think about the religious beliefs that were common to some people at that stage. Erm, most of Britain, most of England, was Protestant, and 25
most of Ireland, in particular the poor people, were Catholic, and certain evangelical extreme Protestants thought that the Famine and the suffering of these people was an act of God, to punish them for being Catholic. And so, they, from that point of view, it would make them also unsympathetic. Now, to be fair, it was really only a small number of people who thought like that, but it was, 30
nevertheless, it, it was a strand of belief at that stage.

And then the final very general underlying reason why help was not very forth-

coming from many people in Britain was, er, the effect of stereotyping, I think you could call it. Over the years, the Irish had been, well, the poor Irish, had been, er, shown in newspapers and in music-halls and things as being lazy, people   35
who had too many children, weren't particularly hard-working, were ungrateful anyway when you gave them help. Erm, in fact, some of the cartoons in the news-papers actually portrayed them as almost sub-human, as like animals, monkeys or something, and so, the general effect of that, also, meant that people were not particularly sympathetic to the plight of the starving millions in, in, in Ireland.   40

TASK 3.4

The fourth extract

So, whatev..., this, the cumulative effect of this is that the help that was sent was in many cases only very half-hearted. For example, food was imported to Ireland, to, as a, grain was imported from America, to take the place of the potatoes, but, either the people had to pay for it, and there were precious few who were able to pay for it of course, or, for the really poor ones, they had to work for it. So, some   5
schemes of what was called Public Works were set up, whereby the people would do some work, and they would get paid in food. Er, the kind of work they'd be asked to do would be building roads, things like that, and they'd have to do it for ten hours a day, on an empty stomach of course, in many cases. But, obviously, there is a limit to the number of roads and bridges and things you can build in a   10
small, a small country, and so in the end, they'd reached the stage where there was no real work to be done, it was just m..., knocking, b... breaking stones up. I mean, ten hours of breaking stones up a day, in order to get some, probably not very good food. You can imagine how demoralising that was for the people who were actually doing the work, and equally, you can see how they weren't putting   15
their heart and soul into this extremely meaningless work. Again, reinforcing the stereotype that the Irish labourer was lazy.

A second way in which they tried to help people was they set up soup kitchens. Erm, mind you, the soup was fairly watery and not particularly nourishing, erm, but at the height of the, the Famine, there was three million people a day, and   20
remem... remember it's out of a population of eight and a half million, three million people a day who we... were being fed by the soup kitchens. But, again, they didn't want the population to become too dependent on these soup kitchens, so they only lasted a short time, only lasted for a few months at, at the height of the Famine. I mean, you can see again and again the parallels to   25
people's attitudes to the famine in Ireland and the attitude to people have about famine in Africa today. In many ways it's really quite interesting.

Erm, following on from soup kitchens, there was a thing that was particularly repugnant to people's ideas nowadays, I think. There was a thing called souperism, whereby the people were promised more food or, or rather offered   30
more food, if they would convert, if they would change their religion from

Catholicism to Protestantism. Now, again, you have to remember it only, occurred in a small pop... a small proportion of cases, it was not widespread, but it did occur in some cases, and you can imagine the effect that that would have on people. I mean, here they are starving to death, and being told, 'Well, OK, if 35 you change your beliefs, or if you say you've changed your beliefs, we'll give you some food.'

The final resort for people who were absolutely and totally destitute was what was called the workhouse. This was just a great, big barn, a great, big building full of people who were very close to death. Basically, you either went there 40 because you were dying or you went there knowing that you would die pretty soon, because of course they were full of disease, full of illness. I mean, nothing could be done to help the people there. So obviously people were very, very reluctant to go there because they saw it as their, their death.

So, all in all, the success of any a... a... attempts to help, to, to deal with the star- 45 vation and the suffering of the people, these attempts met with only very limited success.

Task 3.5

The final extract

So, what option did the people have? Really, they couldn't stay, so the obvious thing to do for many of them was, to leave their native country and emigrate somewhere else, and the obvious place to go at that time, the middle of the eigh- teen, 1800s, was Canada or America. It's estimated that about one and a half million people from Ireland emigrated to Canada and America at that time. Erm, 5 that's on top of the one million we've already said who died of starvation and disease at the time. They went because they hoped that they would find a better life there. They, they'd seen their family, their friends, dying of starvation. They went to the west of Ireland, they paid their last remaining life savings to get a passage on a boat and sailed across to the better life they hoped they were going 10 to. But, in fact, many of them didn't even reach their 'better life', many of them died on the boats because the boats were so overcrowded. The people arrived on, arrived on the boats full of disease as well, and, in fact, the boats were called 'coffin ships' because so many died en route to America and Canada.

So, you have to imagine these people and, and the ideas, the beliefs, the feelings, 15 the emotions they're taking with them as they go to Canada and America. Of course, they'll see Britain and the English as the oppressors, as the people who watched while millions of men, women and children were starved to death. And, of course, many of them felt very, very bitter towards the, the British. And they took these ideas with them when they went to America, and, the ideas lived in 20 their memories and became almost part of the folk tradition of American, of many Americans. Erm, and you've got to remember that many people in America now do claim to be of Irish descent. I mean, there's, there's even politicians, even presidents, who make a great thing of being of Irish descent.

And this anti-British feeling has uh.., in fact still colours a lot of feelings that   25
Americans have about the British today. So we can see from all of this that
although the Famine took place 150 years ago, it still affects how people view
each other today, in today's world.

Unit 7, Task 1.2

Food in Britain (12′58″): The first extract

O.K. well, I want to talk to you about food in Britain. Roughly speaking, I want
to talk about three bits to you. I want to give you something of an introduction,
I then want to talk a bit about food in Britain historically, and then I want to
talk about what the present situation is like.

All right then, let's start at the beginning. Well, what do we eat anyway? Well,   5
there are four factors, I think. We eat what is available you know. If it isn't there,
you can't have it, and that may sound very obvious but it's quite clearly part of
the situation. Secondly, we eat what we can afford. It may be there but we can't
afford to buy it. So that's another important factor. What do we eat then? What
we trust to be wholesome and nutritious. Again, we may not eat it; we may not   10
be able to, er, we may be able to afford it but we decide not to eat it because we
don't think it's right to eat, even though it is available. And perhaps, fourthly, we
eat because we think we're going to enjoy it. Don't forget, there's a lot of pleasure
in eating food, and, so one shouldn't deny that. We don't just eat in order to
build our bodies, or whatever it is, or because we're hungry. Hopefully, we're well   15
enough off to be able to eat because we enjoy eating. So it's quite a complex situation, our relationship with food.

So what do we find that the British eat? Well, quite clearly, they can only eat
what is available to them, and again, it depends on what they can afford, how
affluent a country it is, what are the relative costs of the different foods within   20
the country. And then of course it depends on current ideas. So these things
obviously apply to any of us and they would apply to any other society.

Now these four factors that I've mentioned are not independent but they are
interrelated, and they need to be viewed in a historical context. One needs to,
say, ask the question, well, why is it like that here?   25

Unit 7, Task 2.1

The second extract

So I want to move on to the second topic now, the historical part, but it isn't really just history. I want to talk about three aspects. I want to talk about the geography, the population we have, and the climate. They all have an effect on what we eat. Well, first of all, let's look at the geograph... geographical situation. Er, Britain is an island. Er, it's an island off the west coast of Europe. Because it's an island, it has sea all the way round. Because it has sea all the way round, i..., the temperature tends to be stabilised. It may not feel like that, but certainly the temperature's much more stable than it would be, er, otherwise. But in addition to that, there's also the Gulf Stream. Now, the Gulf Stream originates, er, in the West Indies, and comes right across the Atlantic, bearing, er, relatively warm, er, sea, er, with it, and that warm sea, er, certainly improves our temperature, i... increases our temperature, not only in this country, er, but also further north in Norway. We're particularly lucky in that respect, because the sea is therefore warmer than it would normally be at this sort of latitude.

Well, because of our favourable situation, we have had quite a succession of peoples living here. As far as we know, er, the Celts were the first population that arrived in this country, er, the Romans invaded, er, so did the Saxons, and then the Vikings, and the Danes, and the Normans. Don't forget more recently, we've had political and religious, er, refugees in this country, er, people like the Huguenots, mainly because of, er, political and religious, er, persecution on the continent. The same would apply to the Jews – we've had quite a lot of Jews come to this country over the years. We've had a lot of Poles come to this country, particularly at the beginning of the last war, and that flow of peoples into the country is still continuing. There's a lot of interchange, er, with the Commonwealth in particular. A lot of West Indians came to this country, er, many Pakistanis. And that sort of movement of peoples is by no means at an end. It continues, and of course, it has an effect on what our ideas are, what foods to eat, and how we eat the foods and so on. The country, of course, is also well positioned for trade, er, partly because of the sea of course, and for conquest, and the conquest has worked both ways, both outwards and inwards, and so, of course, the Empire grew up, and the particular relations which Britain had with the Empire, and of course subsequently with the Commonwealth.

Well, that's very quickly running over the geographical elements in our situation. But I now want to go on a bit more about the population.

UNIT 7, TASK 3.4

The third extract

Well, as soon as you think about population, you obviously need to think about the area of the country in relation to the population. Well, the current population is about sixty million. And it has been steady for quite a while in spite of the traffic I've talked about, both outwards and inwards. Sixty million people are living in this country, and the important thing to appreciate, is that we can't feed sixty million people with the amount of food which we grow here. That's very important. Clearly we have to import some extra food. And so our trade in food is a most important consideration, and that's why I've put these figures up on the board. Well, it takes a bit of time to just have a look, er, at those figures. Perhaps the best thing to do is to look at the total at the bottom. Well, you can see from those figures, that we export only about half as much as we import, so the balance of trade is very much, in terms of food, is very much, er, against this country. But the interesting thing, I think, is that there's such a big trade in food. If we don't grow enough food in this country to feed ourselves, it's surprising that we should export as much as we do. The figures, incidentally, leave out beverages, and as far as beverages are concerned, we do actually export more than we import, and that's very largely due to whisky. It's quite interesting, that in terms of exports, the total food and drink exports are about 7% of the total, and in terms of imports, food, and foo...er, and drink, represent about al... almost 10% of the figure. So the trade in food and drink is an important tr... part of the total trade of this country. It raises an important question. Are we self-sufficient in food? And, of course, as I've already told you, we can't grow enough food. And it's interesting to know, that we're only about fifty-odd per cent self-sufficient. So we really depend on food coming in from abroad, er, to almost 50%. Now there is another question one can ask in relation to this, because there are foods which we can grow in this country, and one can ask the question of, to what extent are we self-sufficient in those foods which we can grow ourselves. Well the answer to that is, to the extent of about 70%. So, even of the foods which we can grow, about 30% comes in from abroad. Now of course other countries, er, vary very greatly. Er, one can have all sorts of extremes, er, countries like Australia, er, will produce a very high proportion of their own food, and will also, er, export a very large proportion of what they can grow. If you take other countries, er, I visited Abu Dhabi not too long ago, well there the co..., situation is completely the opposite. That's a country which can virtually grow, er, no food at all, so, virtually all the food, er, which i... er, they consume, has to be imported.

5

10

15

20

25

30

35

Unit 7, Task 4.2

The final extract

Well, so, importing of food is very important to us. And of course we have to import a lot of food because we have a large population. Well, if we go back to the figures, you can see what the trade in food looks like, in more detail. The figures are broken down into different products. Er, it includes, er, different types of food materials. Er, it includes some food materials which we use to make 5 drinks, like coffee, tea and cocoa. But it's not really trade in drinks, it's only the trade in food. And you can see there are big differences, as you run down the figures. You can see that meat and meat preparations, we import considerably more, more than twice as much as we export, whereas in dairy products, the balance is more favourable to this country, but it's still negative. Now again, that's 10 a bit surprising, because, er, as you look about you, we are a very green country, and a country that stays green all the year round, so it's pretty well ideal for, er, having cattle, and therefore having milk. When we go to fish, again, we import considerably more than we export, which again is surprising, as I d... have said that we're an island, we've got sea all the way round us, and yet we don't seem to 15 fish enough fish, in order to supply all the needs of this country.

For cereals, we do actually export more than we import. But you should note, that we also have to e..., import quite a lot of cereals, as animal feedstuffs, and those figures are not included. So we do actually import more cereals in total, if you include animal feeds, er, than we export. Tropical fruits, well, quite obvi- 20 ously, our climate is not tropical, so we can't grow them, and so of course we have to import them. Sugar, again, quite a lot of sugar in the world comes from suger cane, and cane is a tropical crop, which we can't grow in this country, we're dependent on sugar beet, but that does not supply the total amount we require. Now again, exported material from this country, is quite often a re-export, rather, 25 er, than something which is truly grown and manufactured in this country. This obviously applies, er, to the tea, coffee and cocoa, er, which we export.

Overall, what I've tried to describe to you is the complexity of the situation. As soon as you start talking about food, it is something which is very complex indeed, involves all sorts of factors, and it's very difficult to come to clear, t..., er, 30 conclusions. But what I've tried t... to explain to you is what the situation in Britain is like, at least in, with some of the main features.

Unit 8, Task 1. 1

The ideas of Milner (1'56″)

Er, good morning everyone. Right. Today, we're going to carry on looking at historical ideas and tracing their origins, and their effects. Er, we'll look particu- larly at the ideas of Milner, and especially at the way he affected, erm, although some might say he failed to affect, er, when we think what's happened in recent years, er, how he affected, erm, anyway his stogglement on developments in the seventies and eighties.   5

I think first, er, we should look at what he achieved in terms of his stogglement on the American permilt, then we'll move on to consider how Britain and, erm, to a lesser extent, continental Europe, tried to implement his ideas. Over the next two lectures we'll be considering the situation in Japan and other countries in   10
Asia with moobling permilts, and we'll be paying particular attention to the diffi-culties that Malaysia, Thailand, and of course Indonesia, faced at the very end of the nineties.

So, Milner. Jay Milner was the first to push the view that traders should be left to get on with it, and be entirely trantable for the outcome of their actions. He   15
supported dingleness, and had no time for shingers, as he called those who lacked courage. He advocated that the only form of control should be a six-monthly review of performance, and he was quite opposed to the hegical forms of control, arguing they robbed traders of the gabbability they needed to maximise opportunity.   20

UNIT 8, TASK 2. 2

Learning and remembering (11′38″): The first extract

I'm going to talk about two ways of looking at the concept of attention. Erm, the first way is, er, seeing attention as being like a torch, and the other view is of attention, erm, being part of short-term memory.

First of all, let's look at the idea of attention being like a torch. Let's think about the metaphor here, just for a moment. Er, imagine that you are, are shining a   5
torch into an otherwise dark room, with no lights. Er, wh... what can you see, and what can't you see? Well, what you can see is what, what is actually in line, in the line of the torch, what is actually, erm, er, being lit up by the torch. What you can't see is everything that's outside the beam of the torch. So the idea of this theory, is that attention is about focusing on things, and ignoring other things.   10
And when you are focusing on one thing, you are completely ignor.., ignoring everything else.

Er, and so we could see this for example, in visual, erm, contexts. For example, erm, imagine the situation where you are meeting a stranger at a station. Erm, you don't know this person but you, you're going to meet them, you've been   15
given a description of their clothes, you know that they're going to be wearing a grey suit. You've been given other information about them, erm they will be carrying a copy of *The Times*, erm, they will have, erm, a certain flower in, in their button hole, erm, and you have to try and identify this person when you go and meet them at the station.   20

Now, according to the theory, what you will be doing when you are trying to identify the person is, you'll be focusing on any examples of the things you're looking for. So, you'll be, you'll be basically focusing on grey suits, copies of *The Times*, erm, flowers, and that kind of thing. Er, in a sense, you'll be seeing those things, but you, you, in a sense, you will not be seeing other things. So you're focusing on those things, erm..., and completely ignoring, and not seeing, and in   25
a sense not perceiving anything else.

We can also see this, erm, in the context of a party conversation. Imagine that you're at a party, erm, the room is full of people, they're all having conversations at the same time. Now, you're taking part in one conversation and you're able to focus on that conversation and you're able to completely ignore all the others,   30
even though the level of noise, er, might be the same from other conversations. You might find other people having their conversations are just as loud as the one that you're having. But you're still able to focus on your conversation and, in a sense, ignore the other conversations. And this might be, er, conceived as hearing, hearing and not hearing. You are hearing the conversation that you're   35
part of, and you are, in a sense, not hearing the other conversations in the room.

So the basic idea of the theory, is that you are processing what you are focusing on, whether you are seeing it or hearing it, and you are not processing what you're not focusing on, you're not seeing it or you're not hearing it.

So the question arises here, what happens to what is ignored? Well, according to   40
this theory, clearly, what is ignored is not processed. Er, and this is where the second theory comes in. The second theory sees attention as being part of short-term memory. And the theory is related to theories of, about how memory is used in general. Er, all cognitive processes involve use, the use of memory. Erm, and there ar..., basically is a fundamental distinction between what's called long-   45
term memory and what's called short-term memory. Long-term memory is used to hold things in memory for long periods of time, for example, erm, your own name, erm, your own telephone number, erm, the information about your mother's face, all of these things are in your memory for a long time and they're part of long-term memory. Short-term memory is the part of memory that's used   50
to process new things. So, sounds that you hear, language that you hear or that you read, erm, things that you see, erm, all of these, erm, these processes of, of seeing or hearing or, or reading these things, involves the use of memory, erm, and involves the use of short-term memory.

Let's take a, an example of a new telephone number. Erm, if you are, erm, you   55
read a new telephone number and you're going to use it, you use short-term memory to keep it, er, in your mind until you've actually dialled the number. In fact, what you're doing is you're mentally repeating the number in your head, erm, repeating it in short-term memory, so that you can keep it available, and then you can dial it. When you've dialled the number, you then have two choices. You can   60
either, erm, forget the number completely, in which case it just goes from short-term memory and then goes, erm, well it just goes out of your head. Er, or, you

can put it into long-term memory. And the way you might do that is perhaps to repeat it a few more times, think about it a bit more, er, and then it might go into long-term memory. Er, so, in the..., the theory basically is saying that short-term 65 memory is the active part of long-term memory, that is to say that, that basically you've got one memory, but it's divided into short-term memory and long-term memory. And short-term memory is the active part of long-term memory. It's what you're thinking about, erm, or perceiving, erm, right now.

So, erm, within short-term memory, you have attention. And attention is the 70 part of short-term memory that is in focus. We could see the relationship between long-term memory, short-term memory and attention, as being like three concentric circles. The outside circle is long-term memory, the ins... , the next inner circle is short-term memory, which is the active part of long-term memory, and then, inside that, we have another circle which is attention, and 75 that's the part of short-term memory that is in focus. What this means is that something can be active, erm, i.e. in short-term memory and therefore being processed, but not being focused on, not in the focus of attention. We may have the impression that what we are not focusing on is ignored, but it is not 80 completely ignored. So, if we are going back to the original examples, for example, the stranger at the station or the, the conversations at the party, we might say that, erm, at the station, erm, you are, you are seeing, erm, grey suits and y.., and you're focusing on them. You may not be, you may not be focusing on black suits, for example, but you are still seeing them, you're still processing 85 them in some way. And in the party conversations, you are actually processing the, the other, erm, conversations that you're not interested in, even though you're not focusing on them. And this is the real difference between the two theories. Er, and the possibility with the second theory is that something that is not in focus, but is active, i.e. in short-term memory, is available for processing. 90 It's not completely ignored, and you can do something afterwards with that information.

UNIT 8, TASK 2. 5

The second extract

OK, let's consider an example of that. Erm, I'll talk about a psychological experiment that involved reading comprehension. I won't go into the details of, erm, the people who did this now. You'll find a reference on your reading list that I gave you at the beginning of term. Basically, the experiment involved people reading a text about an old l..., house in the country. Two different groups were 5 asked to read the text. One group was told, 'You are thinking about buying a house, and we would like you to read the text and, and consider this house, and whether it might be the kind of house that you might want, might want to buy.' This group we can call the house buyer group. The second group were told, 'You are burglars, you are people who steal things from houses. We would like you to 10 read this text about a house and think about, erm, this house and how, erm, as a burglar, you might, erm, think that this mi... , this house might be one that you could burgle.'

So, what happened after that? Well, each of the groups read the text, and afterwards they were given a recall task. They were asked to remember everything 15
they could about the text. In the house buyer group, the summaries basically concentrated on information that might be useful to house buyers. For example, information was given about the size of the rooms, er, the state of the roof, the decoration, erm, about the carpets, for example. With the group of burglars, their summaries, erm, concentrated on things that were useful to burglars, for 20
example, the details of the alarm, the type of security arrangements, the locks on the windows, the type of doors, that kind of thing. Now all this is not very surprising. It's, it's more or less as you would expect. I mean, the house buyer group was asked to focus on things that might be useful to house buyers and so it's not really a surprise that they, these things were in their summaries. But what 25
is surprising is what the, erm, what was done next in the experiment.

There was a second recall task, and the groups were asked to switch perspectives. The house buyer group was told, 'OK, that was your summary, that's fine. Erm, we want to see whether you can add any more information to that summary. Erm, we'd like you to imagine now that you are a burglar, who might be inter- 30
ested in, in burgling this house.' And, again, with the other group, the burglar group were told, 'OK, you've done that summary. We'd like you to see if there's any more information that you can remember about the text. Erm, but this time, erm, imagine that you're a house buyer who might be interested in buying the house'. And basically, more information was given by the two groups. And, in 35
fact, the group that was originally the house buyer group, that was now asked to concentrate on remembering anything else that might be relevant to a burglar, came up with information that was relevant to burgling the house. And the other group, that, that originally was the burglar group but was, but which was now asked to consider things that might be useful to a house buyer, came up with 40
some more details that might be useful to a house buyer. And what you have to remember is that they, they didn't read the text again for this. This was all done on the same, on on the original reading. They weren't reading the text again.

Erm, so what this suggests, is that each group were able to add new things, erm, that they weren't able to recall the first time they were asked to do the recall task. 45
Which means that there were things in the input that were processed, erm, but not focused on, and afterwards, readers were able to get that information, er, and remember it, even though they hadn't been able to remember it initially when they did the, the, their first summary of the text. Now, this seems to provide, er, empirical support for the second of the two theories, erm, that is the idea of 50
attention being part of short-term memory in focus, because it allows this possibility that information can be active, i.e. in short-term memory, erm, a... and therefore not in focus of attention, but still might be useful for later. Some recall of this unattended input is possible, it's not completely ignored.

Cassette 3, side 1
Unit 8, Task 3.3

Thomas Kuhn (10'05")

I'm going on today to another topic, and that's talking about Kuhn, Thomas Kuhn. Erm, I haven't got a handout this time, but if you look at the one I gave you last week – yes? – you'll see that it's got the er, reading list on it, and I'll be coming back to that later on.

Kuhn was of course, a historian and philosopher of science. Erm, he died in 1996, June 1996. It was surprising that so little attention was given to his er, his passing away, because he was a man who'd made a huge impact in his time, an enormous stir with his ideas, back in the '60s. Anyway, let's take things back, to the beginning. Erm, we'll go back to the 1940s, when Kuhn was teaching at Harvard University. One of the things he had to do at that time, was to teach a science course to a, a humanities class. Now that, as you can imagine, is not an easy task. So, Kuhn sat down to think about it and to prepare, and his reading took in – amongst a lot of other things –some of the works of Aristotle. Aristotle, as I'm sure you know, erm, was one of the most important ancient philosophers, and Kuhn sat and thought about Aristotle's notions of motion and matter.

Now, according to some observers, Aristotle had what has been described as a fairly 'common sense' view of nature. He thought that any body, such as a, a rock or a cart or something of the sort, will remain at rest unless an external force moves it. For example, if you throw a rock, it hits the ground, and if you push a cart, it stops when you stop pushing it any further. So, according to Aristotle, when a body comes to rest, it finds its natural place in the universe. And that seemed a very common sense sort of understanding.

Now, along comes Newton at the end of the 17th century, and what does Newton suggest? He says no no no no no, the natural state of bodies is not in fact one of rest, it's actually one of motion, and rest, or zero velocity, is an exception to that norm of motion. So, says Newton, a body will continue in a state of rest or moving along a straight line in a state of uniform motion unless and until impacted on by some force. And that, as I'm sure you'll recognise, is Newton's first law of motion. The action of the force will change the motion.

So, Newton's system replaced Aristotle's, er and incidentally, this is another example of something I drew attention to last week – which, if you remember, was the er, essentially false notion that science is 'nothing but trained and organised common sense'. You'll remember that that was a view put forward by er, among others, T.H.Huxley in the 19th century. I'll come back to that later on. But what I really want to look at at this point, are the observations that Kuhn made about Aristotle and Newton. These were observations that were eventually to lead to his groundbreaking, absolutely revolutionary ideas. The question that Kuhn was interested in was, 'Why was Newton's system so radically different

5

10

15

20

25

30

35

from Aristotle's?' I mean, you only have to think about it, don't you, here are two
systems so radically different, they seem worlds apart. Aristotle's idea, that every-   40
thing has a natural place, just has no room in Newton's scheme of things. Er and,
what room is there in Aristotle's view for Newton's ideas of a natural state of
motion?

Well then. One could argue, fairly convincingly, that Aristotle's ideas were primi-
tive. They did, after all, come at the very dawn of science in the 4th century BC.   45
But Kuhn wondered; why, if some of Aristotle's ideas in philosophy or ethics, for
example, if these ideas continue to command such high respect in the modern
world – which they certainly do – then why are his notions of matter and
motion so outmoded? Why do they seem almost laughably simplistic? What,
asked Kuhn, could have made Aristotle put forward ideas about matter and   50
motion in the form that he did?

Well, the answer, Kuhn suggested, was that Aristotle was working in a collectively
established framework of ideas called a paradigm. What this means is that
Aristotle's ideas fitted in very well with the prevailing paradigm of scientific
concepts in his time. This paradigm presented apparently satisfactory explana-   55
tions of the world and so they went unchallenged. Unchallenged for a very long
time in fact – after all they were still around in the Middle Ages.

The important thing that Kuhn observed was that no explanation is completely
satisfactory. Any theory may have a chink, or an anomaly, whatever you want to
call it. A sort of hole in it. And then eventually what happens is that this, this   60
hole grows, there's increasing dissatisfaction with the existence of the anomaly
and so there's increasing pressure to try to resolve it. When there's enough pressure, a kind of crisis will arise, and everyone starts to question the existing paradigm, the existing framework. Well, eventually somebody comes up with a more
satisfactory explanation, and that, of course, is what Newton did at the end of   65
the 17th century. As this new explanation takes hold, we get this thing that
Kuhn labelled a paradigm shift –it's like a, a scientific revolution, which was in
fact the term he used in the title of his book, *The Structure of Scientific
Revolutions*. Erm that came out in the 1960s, erm, 1962 to be exact.

Kuhn suggested that the way scientific enquiry operates is not a completely   70
objective, value-free, rational one, which is what some scientists undoubtedly
believe it to be. He suggested that scientific enquiry occurs within prevailing
paradigms and those working within them might, it seems, be unaware, actually
not realise, that these paradigms are essentially provisional, they're provisional
explanations of the world, and one day they could be replaced or improved   75
upon. What's more, the attraction of a particular paradigm might depend on
non-scientific factors I suppose, such as certain aesthetic qualities, or perhaps
compatibility with religion, erm with religious explanations of the world.

Now this idea of Kuhn's opened up a real Pandora's box of controversy and I
must say, misunderstanding. It wouldn't be an exaggeration to suggest that   80

Kuhn's concept has been one of the most misunderstood ideas of our time. It has, for example, led some people to the view that you can ignore all the factual evidence that belonged to an old paradigm, and of course this has been shown not to be the case. Of course you can't do that. If that were true, then you'd have to see Aristotle's system as being completely unrelated to Newton's, but that's not actually how it is. The Newtonian revolution certainly didn't sweep away all Aristotle's notions of motion and matter. For instance, there was no radical change in the notions of structures of space and time and erm, what constitutes a material body – those things remained largely unchanged in Newton's explanations. 85

90

Now of course, it has to be said that as with many controversial, groundbreaking theories, Kuhn's was a bit of a two-edged sword. On the one hand it has led, I think, to people imagining new paradigms when there's no justification at all for it. In other words, I think the concept's been rather widely abused. But, on the other hand, it has contributed to what I think is a very valid questioning of the way that scientists operate. There is no longer a blind acceptance of the view that scientists are totally objective. 95

UNIT 9, TASK 2.1

Water (14′49″)

Introduction

I'm going to be talking today about water, farms and farming, and with a title about water the obvious opening statement is to hope that you do have a thirst for knowledge of this kind, as listeners, which I can at least partly satisfy.

I want to try to link these three terms of water, and farms, and farming together, by taking the idea of water as a resource. It's a resource which can be put directly to use for conversion to human food or fibre or fuel or raw materials for industry, because although you need some other things, er, notably carbon dioxide it is a fact that water in a plant contributes to much more complicated molecules, and in that way is something very useful to human life. I'm going to ignore the undoubtedly important role of water in life generally, and in industry, and as a source of hydro-electric power and in transport and even in hygiene, and I'm going to discuss the idea of water as a resource for farms and farming, at a rather general level. 5

10

The structure of the talk is quite simple. I'll take the terms one after the other. I'll start with water, and say something about its qualities, and this is going to need a bit of self-discipline, because it's such interesting stuff that one could simply spend the entire time available simply talking about what is water. And then I'll move on to farms, and I want to take the line that the most important thing about a farm is not the farm in fact, but the farmer. In other words, it's not 15

farms that produce commodities and it's not farms that have problems – it's   20
farmers who actually organise production in their area of land, and it's the
farmers who therefore have the problems, and they have to attempt to solve
them. And then I'll talk about farming which is, to come to the point of the
matter, the ways in which water is actually used as an input for production and,
of course, in many ways, water is no different from any other input – for   25
example, you could argue, quite easily I think, that water is simply a fertiliser,
and you can think about it in that way.

Section 1: The qualities of water

Let's start with water, and let's limit ourselves to three obvious, but very important, characteristics of this stuff. First of all, it's one of the few things in the
world which exist as a solid, and as a gas, and as a liquid. As a solid, in fact, we
keep most of it refrigerated, and some 80% of the non-oceanic water in the
world is held in a very nice, refrigerated condition at both the north and south   5
pole. As a gas, if you like, as a vapour, it has probably one of its most important
functions – and that is, that it serves as the heat regulator for the whole globe.
The oceans are ways in which heat is stored; otherwise it would be released into
the terrestrial parts of the world and we would all experience a very much higher
temperature. But because we have this huge heat reservoir, occupying some two-   10
thirds of the globe, and because the water then evaporates, it's a mechanism for
controlling the whole heat system in the globe. And finally as a liquid, that's
quite obvious – the interesting point there perhaps is that some 97% of the water
is salty, in the seas, and it's only some 3% in the world which actually exists as
fresh water. The second point to note is that water cycles, that's to say, it transfers   15
between these three conditions of solid, and gas and liquid. Now this has been
known a very long time. There are descriptions going back to some 500 B.C. in
which the scientists of the day speculated about the ways in which water in rivers
and seas and clouds were related. Unfortunately, they got it the wrong way
round, and the general ancient view was that the sea forces its way up through   20
the land, up through the rivers, up into the sky, and then falls down again, and it
was rather later that the right way of cycling, that is to say, evaporation from the
seas and oceans into clouds, and then down onto the land, that the thing was got
the right way round. Well, the other, or at least another interesting point about
its cycling behaviour, is that of course the total amount of water doesn't change.   25
As far as we know, water does not escape into the outer atmosphere, and as far as
we know, very little is coming up from the interior of the earth so what we have,
is a finite amount of water which changes around through the various forms, in
different parts of the world, in this cycling fashion. In fact, the calculation is,
that something like a layer of water, about a metre deep, over the entire globe   30
circulates every year. Just in passing, incidentally, more of that water falls as rain
on the oceans than it does on land, of course, and that makes its use by people
directly rather more difficult. Well the third point to note about water, is that
things dissolve in it, not only the sugar in our tea or coffee, but in moving

through the soil, it collects salts, and sometimes those salts in the water can   35
become a nuisance. They may in fact affect our drinking water. It also, of course,
carries things not totally dissolved in it but simply suspended in it, things like
small soil particles or silt, and that of course has very important implications for
people in river deltas, and is very much concerned with the story of human civilisation, in earlier centuries. Just as water dissolves things in it, sometimes it's   40
important to remove the water, and so whilst thinking of water and what it does
in a positive sense, one does have to remember that sometimes we have too much
of it and drainage then becomes the issue.

Section 2: Farms, farmers and the need for local organisation of water

Let's move on to farms, and note first of all, that the use of water in some kind of
irrigation system is extremely ancient. There are examples of irrigation schemes
going back to something like 4000 BC. It's helpful, of course, that the water used
on farms doesn't have to be clean. The crops don't mind if it's a bit dirty, and of
course, you don't need it all the time, you only need it when the crops are   5
growing. One of the very ancient systems of getting water on farms was simply
to allow the land to be fallow, to grow nothing, and, in areas of low rainfall, there
are very ancient farming systems where the soil is left fallow for two years or,
sorry, for one year usually, and it only carries a crop every other year, so that
what you're doing really is to use one year to store up water, and then you use, in   10
a sense, two years of supply to grow one year of crop. The other matter, of
course, is some form of irrigation. On farms, perhaps the first thing that a farmer
would say to you, immediately, is that a great deal of work is involved in getting
the water. You have to make channels; you have to keep them clean, you have to
arrange for the shared use of the water by yourself and by the surrounding   15
farmers and all of this requires some kind of local management input and, of
course, usually, some kind of national effort in terms of policy and government
departments whose job it is to try to solve the technical problems of bringing
water to the farmers. The experience we have, I think, of many centuries of
attempts to improve the water supply to farms is that the, er, fundamental   20
process has to be one of using the resources of local people. It has to be based on
self-reliance and learning by the users, it's not something that is easily done by
centralised planning, nor by the actions of technocrats who are far-removed from
the rural areas. So what has happened over many centuries is gradually to understand, that the way to deal with the supply of water at farm level is to bring   25
people together in small, informal local groups to work together, to solve the
problems, er, to organise the supplies, to maintain them and then to join these
little groups together into bigger organisations and associations, so that they can
deal with things at the national level.

Section 3: How water is used in farming

And now farming. Well, there are two sources of water that can be used in the
processes of farming. You can either use surface water, which is that which falls
down at that time from the sky or you can use ground water, which is the water
that's already fallen, and is simply stored in the aquifers and in the materials
under the surface. It's quite easy, if this is used properly, to double crop produc-   5
tion in areas where rainfall is a limiting factor, but we have to remember too that
a raindrop is an explosive. Raindrops bring down energy with them, and when
they hit the ground that energy is released, and the result of that can quite easily
be erosion, and the removal of small particles of soil. So it's always a question of
controlling the explosive action of rain and making the best use of it in the   10
productive sense. There's also associated problems with health. Water supplies, if
they're used in farming, can quite easily increase insect and snail populations and
some of those are associated with very unpleasant human diseases. This can be
balanced, by the way, by creatures nicer to us, ducks, and frogs, that eat pests.
Anyway, there's also problems of soil damage by the salts dissolved in water. If the   15
water moves upwards through the soil, instead of downwards, and evaporates, it
can leave behind a heavy deposit of salt, and this in the end can make soil quite
incapable of growing crops. There's also problems at the level of disputes.
Communities don't always agree easily about who shall have the water, and how
much of it, and when, any more than national governments sometimes can agree   20
about who shall use the major river resources that happen to run through more
than one country.

There are in fact two principles at stake I think when water is used in farming.
The first one is to try to organise a better retention of that water which does fall
and this is a matter of trying to get a good cover of plants on the soil surface, of   25
creating barriers so the water doesn't run away, and having high levels of organic
matter in the soil, to absorb and retain the moisture, and then to find crops to
grow which are best adjusted to the levels of water available, and to manipulate
the planting time to make the best use of the water that does fall. There are lots
of ways of actually dealing with the water in terms of irrigation methods. I   30
suppose we're all familiar with watering cans, and it's everything from that up to
very advanced sprinklers and trickle-feed systems, which are attempts to make
small amounts of water continuously trickle around the roots of individual plants
and, therefore make the best use of that water. And in between all sorts of inter-
mediate kinds of technologies, things like sinking pots, porous pots into the soil   35
so that the water in them gradually leaks into the surrounding soil.

The other principle that's at stake here I think, is the way in which the water is
actually obtained by the plant and there are basically two ways in which this
works. Er, one method is that the water, the rain, falls simultaneously with the
planting of seeds. This is the action of planting at the beginning of a wet season.   40
What subsequently happens is that the water moves down through the soil and
the roots run down after it, chasing it, and you hope capturing as much of the
water as possible before it finally dries out. And you hope the crop will mature

before growth becomes impossible. And over large surfaces of the earth, it's the
root chasing the water. The other system, which is perhaps more typical of   45
countries in north-west Europe, is that during the winter, when the crops are not
grown, the soil acts as a reservoir for the rain that falls, er, so that you have a wet
soil, and a supply of water available to last the crop through the growing season.
It's topped up by rain during growth fortunately, but the principle is that this
water is already available in the soil, you plant your seeds, and the water   50
gradually moves upwards, through a process of trickling upwards, and so the
roots, in theory, get a constant supply of water. Sometimes, indeed, they don't
have to grow very deeply down in order to cope.

Conclusion

Well, now a conclusion. It may well be that when we look around the world at
the state of water and farms and farming, that the conclusion we come to is that
very frequently farm production is not adequately adjusted to the irrigation
potential, and that irrigation practice is not adjusted to the environment. It's this
condition, I think, which characterises much water use in farming and the   5
improvement of this condition needs very careful management. There's much to
be done, and of course, much is being done throughout the world.

Cassette 3, side 2
FURTHER PRACTICE

1. Conflict Management (13'02")

Today's session is called Managing Conflict. This is not a session, particularly, for
managers, despite the title. Conflict exists in all our lives, and we all need to
manage it effectively. So in today's session, we're going to look at conflict, what it
is, and what causes conflict, and even, how conflict can be valuable, how it can
be useful. Then, we're going to look at how to manage conflict, how to actually   5
make the conflict come right for you as a person.

So first, what is conflict? The word can cover everything from a minor disagreement through to an argument, a fight, even a full-scale war. Conflict is everywhere in our everyday lives. Why? Why is there conflict? There are many reasons.
The basic reason is that people are different. They have different politics, they   10
have different religions, they have different ideas about the world, and how to do
things. And, of course, they have different emotions. So, some reasons for
conflict – political, religious, intellectual, emotional.

Conflict is everywhere. Could we imagine a world without conflict? Is that our
ideal situation? Well, let's see. In a world without conflict, we would all have one   15
view of the world. We would all have one idea about how to do something. We
would all have one solution to a particular problem. It's hard to imagine, in a
world like that, that civilisation would make any progress at all. Just to take one

example, the history of science is full of people in conflict, people disagreeing with the current view of the world. If we didn't have disagreement, surely we wouldn't have progress. So, our ideal world is not a world with no conflict. Perhaps our ideal world is a world in which conflict can be used to our advantage, but we can manage it so that it doesn't cause us problems.   20

And how can we manage conflict? Can we perhaps simply avoid it? Is that a good management stru..., er, strategy? Let's see. Most of us don't like the idea of   25
conflict, so it seems reasonable that we should simply avoid conflict at all costs. Let's imagine a case where, er, your partner, or a colleague at work has some kind of annoying habit, something silly maybe, something like the way they drink their coffee. We want to avoid conflict, so we decide to do nothing. Let's investigate that for a moment. If we do nothing, what could happen in that situation?   30
There are three possibilities. First, it could get better. The partner could stop the annoying habit. They could start drinking their coffee the way we drink our coffee, the way we expect coffee to be drunk. Secondly, th..., the situation could stay the same, they could carry on drinking their coffee in that strange way that annoys us so much. Third, the situation could get even worse. It's not just coffee,   35
it's Coca Cola, and tea, and everything else they drink, and then it's everything they eat as well. Everything they do at the dinner table annoys us. So we have three possible scenarios. If we do nothing, things could get better, they could stay the same, or they could get worse. The first point to notice there, is there are two bad results, and only one good one. If things stay the same, we will be very   40
unhappy. If they get worse, we'll be even more happ..., unhappy. The second point to notice is, what is the probability of things getting better? Very small. If your partner doesn't know that the way they drink their coffee annoys you, what is the chance that they will change the way they drink their coffee? Very small. We must somehow make them aware of this cause of conflict. We can't avoid the   45
conflict, it will probably get worse. Indeed, if we think of the, the worst kinds of conflict, actual fighting, and wars, most of these conflicts started as small annoying habits, small annoying behaviour patterns of people, which got worse and worse through a spiral of conflict, with people hardening their positions to each other, with people demonising the other person. Suddenly, the person is not   50
a thinking, rational being any more, but some kind of demon, behaving very very badly. And finally we get to the stage where people pick sides, and we have a full-scale war to deal with. If we don't deal with conflict, if we avoid conflict, it usually gets worse.

However, this does not mean that we have to cause conflict unnecessarily. We   55
can't avoid conflict, but we can avoid confrontation. There are a number of ways we can avoid confrontation. For example, I have a different political view to you, but I don't have to wear a badge to work which shows what political party I support. I don't have to talk to you about my politics, if I don't know you very well. And I don't have to behave in an aggressive way towards you personally.   60
These are all things we can, and should, do, every day of our lives, to avoid confrontation.

So when I talk about conflict management, I do not mean you simply avoid the conflict. I mean you avoid the confrontation in the first place. If you get to a point where a true conflict exists, then you must somehow manage it. How? None of us like to deal with a conflict situation, but there are a few rules which can help to lead to a successful conclusion. If you follow these rules, in my experience, most times the results are very good. First, you must pick the time and the place to deal with the conflict. The dialogue you're going to have with the person is going to have some difficult moments. You don't want it to be interrupted by your mobile phone ringing, or by someone coming into the room. Pick a time and a place where the conversation can continue for as long as it takes. Set the scene, secondly, set the scene. Make sure everyone is sitting comfortably, everyone can see each other, it's possible for everyone to contribute without any difficulty. Thirdly, and very importantly, apologise. You're not apologising for something you've done wrong. Apologise for the fact that the conflict has arisen in the first place. This is very disarming. If you say to someone who you are in conflict with, 'I am sorry we have this problem,' if you begin your conversation like that, that is a very powerful way to start. Immediately, the conversation is on a different footing. So, pick the time and the place, set the scene, and apologise for the fact of the conflict. Fourthly, explain the purpose of the meeting carefully, and fifthly request a statement of the problem as the other person sees it. Listen carefully. Listen actively. When the person has finished, restate the problem. Try to take away all the emotional extras that have been added in the account. O.K. so, request a statement of the problem, listen actively to the statement, and then restate the problem, taking away all the negative adjectives and the value judgements. Try to bring it down to a simple statement of fact. What has happened, which has caused the conflict? Elicit a solution from the other person. What do they see as a possible solution to this conflict? This is the second very powerful part of conflict management. When a person comes in to discuss a conflict, they are full of emotion. Their emotional side is controlling them. You give them a chance to show that emotion by asking them to state the problem, but then, when you ask them for a solution, you're moving away from emotion into rational thought. It is very hard for a person to remain emotional when you're asking them for a rational solution. In my experience, at this point, the conversation changes. The atmosphere of high emotion is replaced by an atmosphere of problem-solving. And now, you can begin to work towards a compromise that solves the conflict. So, pick a time and place, set the scene, apologise, explain, request, listen, restate, elicit a solution. Work towards a compromise. These are the ways, in my experience, of working through a structure, to manage an existing conflict.

To sum up then. Conflict is an essential part of everyday life. It exists, because we are different people. Indeed, it actually helps us to advance in civilisation. But conflict can also destroy, if it is not managed effectively. Learn how to manage conflict effectively, and you will have a much more effective personal and professional life.

FURTHER PRACTICE

2. Archaeology (12'08")

Right, well, I want to say something to you today, about the appeal of archaeology and, er, to look at some of the features which mark various developments in archaeology over, its historical development, erm, and I'm going to take as, as a specific exemplification of these, er, the excavations at Pompeii, in southern Italy, Pompeii and Herculaneum.   5

Well, first of all, er, archaeology. I think most people feel it's a, a fascinating field of study, and some of you will have seen, erm, some of the programmes recently on television, which have attracted huge audiences, a massive following in the country. It does have a, an, an appeal to our imagination.

First of all, when f..., people first began to get, er, interested in archaeology, well,   10
they didn't call it archaeology in those days, it was more like treasure hunting.
People used to, erm, er, dig around looking for, erm, impressive statues and treasures, things like that, things they could sell on the open market. And then, after a while, people became not so much interested in the, in the grand, er, things that they could dig up, but in the, erm, er, in the minutiae of everyday life.   15
People's imaginations were fired. I suppose even with the, er, the large statues and the, and the treasures, they, maybe the major appeal of these, was that, erm, they had been in circulation, er, thousands of years ago, so even then, even with those, the, the appeal was, erm, not only financial but one to the imagination.

Er, But then, er, pe..., as I say, people began to get more interested in finding out   20
what daily life was like in other societies. But still the appeal, imagination, and then, there became an ever-deepening, erm, intellectual side to archaeology, in which the archaeologists theorised about not just how it was in ancient life, but, er, theorising about the structure of ancient societies, why societies took the form they did, and why their physical embodiments took the form they did, erm, and   25
when societies changed and when the nature of towns changed, or whatever, why did the, the towns change in a particular way? And people would set up theories and hypotheses and so on. And we can see some or all of these various, er, phases in archaeology, er, summed up in the two cities of Pompeii and Herculaneum in southern Italy, in, in the Bay of Naples. And I think, erm, maybe many of you   30
will know that, er, in fact it was a, a known day in August in the year 79, that, er, the volcano Vesuvius, in the Bay of Naples, it exploded, and with this explosion, millions of tons of, er, lava and, er, volcanic dust went up into the atmosphere, and lava flowed down from the volcano and sealed in, erm, all kinds, there must have been all kinds of villages and smaller communities, but the ones we know   35
most about, are these two cities, Pompeii and Herculanem, they were trapped, and they were completely covered, two entire cities. And they were lost until the early 1700s, people even forgot that they had existed. But in the early 1700s, pieces of beautifully carved marble began to appear in, in markets and in shops, and merchants were selling them to, erm, aristocratic collectors. And some of   40

these came to the attention of a, a prince, and I don't know what kind of prince
he was, because his name was Elboeuf. Er, but there he was in Italy, but, er, erm,
nevertheless, it came to his attention. And, erm, he wanted to find out where
these wonderful pieces of marble were coming from. And he employed workmen
and found that, er, the source of many of these er, erm, statues, and so on, er,   45
was the city of Herculaneum. Well, actually, it was Ercolano, the Italian city, and
it was discovered there was another city underneath the city, and this was the
ancient city of Herculaneum.

And in about 1720, the Prince of Elboeuf employed his workmen to tunnel into
this ancient city, and it has to be admitted, that what he was after was not, erm,   50
matters of historical interest, really, but pieces of beautiful statuary to adorn his,
er, palaces. So this was an archaeology if you like, an archaeology of precious
objects.

And this was continued by the King and Queen of Naples, who took over the
work. One wonders why they took it over, because, I suppose, er, they wanted to,   55
er, start digging up some of this wonderful stuff as well. But the work became a
little more systematic. Maybe they felt that, er, by more systematic excavations
they would discover more. But in the process of their more systematic work, er,
they extended the work from Herculaneum and they discovered Pompeii in
1748. But their objective, as I say, was still to find ancient masterpieces for their   60
homes.

But, they discovered something for the mind almost immediately. Just after they
discovered Pompeii, they discovered on the outskirts of Herculaneum a splendid
Roman villa, which was absolutely full of statues, and, what was more fascinating
still, an entire library of papyrus rolls, that is the, the books at that time were   65
rolls of this, erm, paper-like material from papyrus. And what a fascinating
prospect. These hundreds of papyrus rolls containing who knew what. But they
couldn't read them, because all of them had been carbonised by the great heat
from the volcano and the volcanic lava and so on. They're still there, the rolls
exist, but at the moment we can't read them. But, who knows, maybe one day,   70
with the technology of the future, it will be possible (a) to unroll them and (b) to
be able to somehow read the writing on the carbonised, er, papyrus.

And this is a, a feature of, er, much archaeology, actually, that much of it has to
wait until we have the technology available and the possibility of waiting is built
in to the archaeology, so very often not, not everything is dug up, not everything   75
is taken away, on purpose. It's left there until we can look at it with more sophis-
ticated technology.

But to go on. In 1763, a German scholar, a very famous German scholar called
Winckelmann, who is, er, sometimes known as the father of German archaeology, he published a letter on the discoveries at Herculaneum. And these   80
published letter..., he had more than one letter, these published letters, were the
beginning of academic publications on archaeology. And with such a beginning

of publication, it was possible for archaeology to become a true academic
discipline. People could refer to the different, erm, letters and other publications.
Huge masses of publications began to appear after that, and at the same time, the   85
publications began to reveal the fact that other things had been discovered apart
from buildings and papyri. The architecture of the buildings themselves was of
great interest. People were fascinated by that. They found in the buildings furniture. And on the walls of the rooms, the complete rooms, there are wall-paintings, beautiful wall, wall-paintings, with perspective, which was thought to have   90
been discovered much, much, much, much later. Statues, etc. etc. And all of
these, these things, the details of the homes, the architecture, the furniture, the
wall-paintings and so on, and the statues, had a massive influence on how people
began to live their own lives, if they had the money to live them that way. So
furniture began to be remade in the old Pompeiian style, and walls were painted,   95
and so on.

Then in 1864, another development. As the excavators were working away,
digging away at the volcanic ash, they, they noted, from time to time, quite large
holes inside the ash. And this was where the bodies of people who'd been caught
by the ash, where the bodies had been, and then had det... deteriorated inside the   100
ash, the ash had solidified, and then in the hole, erm, inside the ash, the bodies
had gradually decayed away and there's nothing left of them except the skeleton.
But the hole is still in exactly the same shape as the body had been. Erm, but
how could we look at it. Well, a man called Giuseppe Fiorelli in 1860, devised a
technique to reveal the bodies by simply using the hole as a mould, and pouring   105
in plaster of Paris, very simple. A simple piece of technology, but it was then
possible to break away the ash, and there you have, would have, a perfect replica
of the person inside. And not only the person inside, but also the clothes that
they were wearing at the time, the hairstyles, everything, was caught by the fine,
er, caught in fine detail by the plaster of Paris.   110

Much more recently, in this century, people have devised a new technique,
instead of using plaster of Paris, using glass fibre, and this will then, er, enable us
to see the bones inside where the body had been, and also any artefacts which it
had been carrying at the time.

And these, er, many people, er, many of you, will have seen, er, pictures, or   115
maybe you've actually been there and seen the actual, er, bodies, or the replicas of
the bodies lying there. And it is very touching. These bodies capture, er, the last
hours and the last minutes, of the life of that city, from two thousand years ago.
You find, for example, a man and a woman clasping each other in death.

In this century, er, in 1924, between 1924 and 1961, Amadeo Maiuri, if I'm   120
pronouncing it correctly, excavated under Pompeii, so this is a new development,
not stopping at the, er, ground level of Pompeii itself, but then finding what
underlay that. So excavating under Pompeii to find earlier versions of the city, to
see how the city had developed. And in a way, I wish they wouldn't, because I
want to keep the city as it was at the moment of its distinction, o..., of its   125

extinction, but it means that what the archaeologists are really concerned with, is not this admittedly rather evocative view of the city as it was at, at a particular time, they're, they're not interested in the physical objects and walls and bricks of the city so much as the ideas which they represent. So, the archaeologists want to find out why the city is the way it is, why, er, it had, what it had been before and how it developed from one form to another.

And finally, in a more recent project, Roger Ling focused on, erm, analysis of one insula, an insula is a, a block of flats, to find, by looking at, er, how the block of flats had changed over time, how the property boundaries had moved, how the walls of rooms had been changed and so on, what this tells us, for example, about social and economic development in Roman towns of the period. So, the, er, intention, once again, is not to look at the insula as it was at a particular time, but to find out what it could tell us about developments in Roman society and Roman, er, living.

Pompeii is the most complete urban excavation ever made. The town plan, er, as it was at the moment of destruction, is clear in many, many, many details. But there are still big chunks untouched, as I told you. They're, these are remaining, er, for later excavation, or some of them are being excavated even now. In fact, Reading University Department of Archaeology has a licence to excavate one of these areas. But, er, the main thought, or one of the major thoughts of these, erm, areas which are awaiting excavation is to leave something for the future. There will always be something more to be interpreted and more to be discovered.

130

135

140

145